# Nice Guys
## Can Get the
## Corner Office

# Nice Guys Can Get the Corner Office

EIGHT STRATEGIES
FOR WINNING IN
BUSINESS WITHOUT
BEING A JERK

RUSS C. EDELMAN

TIMOTHY R. HILTABIDDLE

CHARLES C. MANZ

PORTFOLIO

PORTFOLIO

Published by the Penguin Group

Penguin Group (USA) Inc., 375 Hudson Street, New York, New York 10014, U.S.A. • Penguin Group (Canada), 90 Eglinton Avenue East, Suite 700, Toronto, Ontario, Canada M4P 2Y3 (a division of Pearson Penguin Canada Inc.) • Penguin Books Ltd, 80 Strand, London WC2R 0RL, England • Penguin Ireland, 25 St. Stephen's Green, Dublin 2, Ireland (a division of Penguin Books Ltd) • Penguin Books Australia Ltd, 250 Camberwell Road, Camberwell, Victoria 3124, Australia (a division of Pearson Australia Group Pty Ltd) • Penguin Books India Pvt Ltd, 11 Community Centre, Panchsheel Park, New Delhi – 110 017, India • Penguin Group (NZ), 67 Apollo Drive, Rosedale, North Shore 0632, New Zealand (a division of Pearson New Zealand Ltd) • Penguin Books (South Africa) (Pty) Ltd, 24 Sturdee Avenue, Rosebank, Johannesburg 2196, South Africa

Penguin Books Ltd, Registered Offices: 80 Strand, London WC2R 0RL, England

First published in 2008 by Portfolio, a member of Penguin Group (USA) Inc.

10  9  8  7  6  5  4  3  2  1

LIBRARY OF CONGRESS CATALOGING-IN-PUBLICATION DATA

Edelman, Russ C.

Nice guys can get the corner office : eight strategies for winning in business without being a jerk / Russ C. Edelman, Timothy R. Hiltabiddle, Charles C. Manz.

p.   cm.

Includes index.

ISBN 978-1-59184-209-5

1. Career development.  2. Management—Psychological aspects.  3. Success in business.  I. Hiltabiddle, Timothy R.   II. Manz, Charles C.   III. Title.

HF5381. E34  2008

650. 1—dc22          2008019434

Printed in the United States of America

*Designed by Chris Welch*

THIS BOOK IS DEDICATED
TO THE NICE GUYS OF THE WORLD
AND TO THE PEOPLE
WITH WHOM THEY WORK.

# Contents

## Why Invest Your Time in This Book?

- Because the adage "Nice guys finish last" is simply not true.
- Because the potential of so many people is inhibited by a problem   Nice Guy Syndrome—that can be overcome.
- Because to be *effectively* nice, to be balanced, will take those people to new plateaus.
- Because it will help overly nice guys and their organizations.
- Because respected CEOs and thought leaders shared their strategies on being nice in business.
- Because we surveyed more than 350 nice guys, and the data is undeniable:

  1. 61 percent of those surveyed believe they are too nice at work.
  2. 41 percent of those people would prefer to be *effectively* nice (balanced).
  3. 36 percent of those people surveyed perceive "success-ful" people as balanced.
  4. 50 percent of those surveyed believe their managers are overly nice.

- Because the cost of being "too nice" is real for both nice guys and their companies.

# Nice Guys
## Can Get the
# Corner Office

Are you a nice guy? Do you work with any nice guys?

If you are like 61 percent of the people in our survey, you identify yourself as a nice guy who is frequently "too nice at work." And if your organization is more than a few people in size, it's a virtual certainty that you are surrounded by nice guys—men and women who are struggling because of their tendency to be "too nice." Let's call these people *overly* nice guys.

What is an overly nice guy?

*Overly nice guys are ubiquitous.* They are everywhere, in all walks of life and in all levels of business. They are men and women, white collar and blue collar; they include all races, ages, and education and income levels. And they all share a common theme: a strong tendency to be "nice" combined with the ongoing frustration they experience when their niceness gets in the way of their success in business and in life.

*Overly nice guys are hardworking.* They are achievers who tend to be diligent and conscientious. Their tendency to be "eager to please" means they'll often go above and beyond the call of duty when something (or someone) is important to them. They take satisfaction from achievement and doing good work, and can be a valuable asset to your organization.

1

*Overly nice guys are struggling.* They need help. Because they're so eager to please, they tend to go overboard—doing what others want them to do, but ignoring their own needs and priorities. This leaves them feeling exploited, frustrated, and overworked.

*Overly nice guys can learn, grow, and change.* They are sensitive and aware, and usually quite open to feedback—sometimes to a fault. Most overly nice guys are easy to coach, mentor, and train, due to their willingness to please others.

*Overly nice guys have huge, untapped potential.* They can be much more effective and productive than they are. With a little training and guidance, they can learn to stick up for themselves, be more effective, and achieve more success.

*Overly nice guys suffer from Nice Guy Syndrome.* Left to their own devices, overly nice guys will continue to struggle with Nice Guy Syndrome. The good news is that the challenges faced by overly nice guys are common and correctable. That's what this book is about.

## How Do We Define "Nice"?

We think it's important to redefine the word "nice." "Nice" includes many positive attributes, including kindness, morals, fairness, common sense, compassion, empathy, ethics, selflessness, and sincerity. It is *not* about being weak or soft.

We consider someone to be "overly nice," however, when he or she shows a tendency toward weakness, "wimpiness," passivity, softness, and docility. By contrast, the "SOB," or jerk, personifies aggression, selfishness, intimidation, narcissism, and impatience.

Extreme leanings toward either of these attributes can limit one's effectiveness. On the one hand, if you are too selfless, you may fail to protect your interests and forsake financial rewards

## Nice

### OLD DEFINITION

A conditioned, well-intentioned approach to relationships that is built on

- Always trying to please others
- Valuing agreeableness over assertiveness
- Treating others "well" by giving away our own personal power
- Prioritizing and catering to others' demands and wants over truthfulness and authenticity
- Attempting to avoid and minimize disagreement, conflict, and discomfort

### NEW DEFINITION

A constructive and consciously chosen approach to relationships that is founded on

- Attempting to optimize outcomes for both others and ourselves
- Striving to balance assertiveness with cooperation to achieve a spirit of collaboration
- Honoring the value and strength of others and ourselves
- Seeking optimal outcomes for everyone involved by emphasizing truthfulness and authenticity
- Openly confronting challenges and disagreements and embracing the innovation-promoting benefits of constructive idea conflict

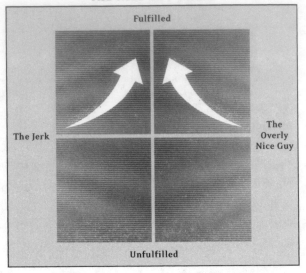

THE NICE GUY GRAPH

and advancement that you deserve; on the other hand, the short-term gains achieved by intimidation, selfishness, and intense aggression frequently lead to long-term failures for the individual and the team. In the long run, learning to find a balance between these two extremes will help the nice guy be more successful and fulfilled in business and in life.

## What about Nice Gals?

Are Nice Gals also Nice Guys? Our use of the word "guys" is not meant to be gender specific. Virtually all the information in this book is directly relevant to both men and women in the business world. In fact, 46 percent of the people surveyed for this book were women.

This is not to say that there aren't specific issues related to women being perceived as too nice, overly nurturing, and of course the diametrical opposite, bitchy. We have observed and heard from many who say there are unique and challenging nice guy issues that are specific only to women. However, as a starting point, this book is intended to be applicable to both genders.

## What Is "Success in Business"?

Some describe business success in terms of money, power, and ambition. Others define it as "making a difference," working on stimulating projects, or achieving a healthy work-life balance. While there are as many definitions as there are people, the bottom line for any individual is: Are my needs—as well as the needs of others—being fulfilled?

In fact, overly nice guys can learn many lessons from jerks, and vice versa. They can adapt in constructive ways. The key to long-term success lies in finding a balance between the extremes of being a jerk and being overly nice. In *Nice Guys Can Get the Corner Office*, we will share a set of practical strategies that will help businesspeople achieve that balance.

## The Nice Guy Strategies (NGS) Bill of Rights

The NGS Bill of Rights consists of eight rights (and corresponding strategies) that can help you and overly nice guys within your organization change perceptions and behaviors, meet challenges, and transcend perceived limitations. If you are overly nice or manage overly nice guys, embracing these rights and learning these strategies will serve you (and them) well. In contrast, if you

# You Have the Right to:

### 1. Self-Awareness

Learn about yourself—know your strengths and weaknesses.

### 2. Speak Up

Learn to express your opinions and be heard.

### 3. Set Boundaries

Learn to set clear, strong, and appropriate boundaries.

### 4. Confront

Learn to confront issues directly and without fear.

### 5. Choose

Learn to make choices without guilt.

### 6. Expect Results

Learn to hold others and yourself accountable.

### 7. Be Bold

Learn to take chances and push the envelope.

### 8. Win

Learn how to finish first respectfully and fairly.

tend toward behaving like a jerk, you are encouraged to reduce the intensity with which you claim these rights. The eight rights are in the box on page 6.

## Whom Did We Interview?

In order to gain additional insights and perspectives for this book, we interviewed numerous CEOs, founders, and thought leaders to supplement, confirm, and challenge our thinking. Collectively, these executives influence and lead in excess of 2.5 million people. Their stories and strategies substantially influenced the content of this book.

**American Cancer Society**—Dr. John Seffrin
*Chief Executive Officer*

**Bell Helicopter**—Terry Stinson
*Former Chief Executive Officer*

**Boston Market**—George Naddaff
*Founder and former Chief Executive Officer*

**Boston Culinary Group**—Joseph O'Donnell
*Founder and Chief Executive Officer*

**Cirque du Soleil**—Daniel LaMarre
*Chief Executive Officer*

**Disney Corporation/Procter & Gamble**—John Pepper
*Chairman of the Board, Disney Corporation*
*Former Chief Executive Officer, Procter & Gamble*

**Dunkin' Brands** (Dunkin' Donuts, Baskin-Robbins)—Jon Luther
*Chief Executive Officer*

**Ernst & Young**—Jim Turley
*Chief Executive Officer*

***Inc.* magazine and Clark University**—George Gendron
*Founder and Director of the Innovation and Entrepreneurship Program, Clark University; former Editor in Chief, Inc. magazine*

***Life is good***—Bert Jacobs
*Cofounder and Chief Executive Optimist*

**Monster.com and Eons.com**—Jeff Taylor
*Founder and former Chief Executive Officer, Monster.com*
*Founder and Chief Executive Officer, Eons.com*

**Outback Steakhouse**—Bill Allen
*Chief Executive Officer*

**Panera Bread**—Ron Shaich
*Founder and Chief Executive Officer*

**Pizzeria Uno**—Aaron Spencer
*Founder, Director, and Chairman Emeritus*

**PricewaterhouseCoopers**—Sam DiPiazza
*Chief Executive Officer*

**Recreational Equipment Inc. (REI) & WRQ Inc.**—Doug Walker
*Chairman of the Board, REI*
*Founder and former Chief Executive Officer, WRQ*

**Southwest Airlines**—Herb Kelleher
*Founder and Chairman of the Board*

**Tweeter Home Entertainment Group**—Joe McGuire
*Former Chief Executive Officer*

**The Vanquard Group**—John Bogle
*Founder and former Chief Executive Officer*

**Washington-Jefferson College**—Dr. Tori Haring-Smith
*President*

**Workplace Relationships Inc.**—Maggie Craddock
*Founder and Chief Executive Officer—Adviser and coach for Fortune 100 CEOs*

**1-800-GOT-JUNK?**—Brian Scudamore
*Founder and Chief Executive Officer*

In addition to these executives, we interviewed and surveyed more than 350 "normal" nice guys who are professionals in different sectors of the business world. Our research helped uncover the many challenges nice guys face in the business world and provided us with stories to illuminate the issues, as well as statistical data from surveys and interviews to provide a quantitative perspective on the many dimensions of the Nice Guy Syndrome.

## The Book's Composition

Each chapter of this book is devoted to one of the eight rights in the NGS Bill of Rights and its corresponding strategies. Within each chapter, we will share stories from normal nice guys to high-ranking executives whom we've interviewed, along with relevant strategies and insights. We have also included statistics from our Nice Guy surveys that highlight key trends and patterns of behavior. Each chapter includes the following:

### NICE GUY SYNDROME: The Challenge

First, we summarize the nice guy challenges associated with each right. This overview provides a glimpse into why nice guys find it difficult to claim that specific right successfully. Each chapter begins with two real-life stories that are related to the specific principle, or right. We have assigned pseudonyms as requested. These stories are gleaned from a wide range of interviews with overly nice guys. After the stories, we discuss the motives for the behavior of the people involved and consider how a nice guy might justify his or her actions. We also identify the key symptoms of the Nice Guy Syndrome for this right and indicate how they can contribute to negative outcomes.

### NICE GUY STRATEGIES: Personal Strategies for Success

We then introduce three personal strategies for each right, including feedback regarding how situations could have been handled more effectively, advice and prescriptions for readers who may experience similar challenges, additional insight and stories from well-known corporate executives and consultants, as well as relevant data from various surveys and interviews. We conclude this section by introducing "Nice Guy Whiplash"—a brief view of what happens when our overly nice guys overreact to situations and how their behavior becomes problematic in the opposite way.

## NICE COMPANY STRATEGIES: Increasing the Effectiveness of Organizations

Finally, we explore the importance of organizations providing healthy support and encouragement of practices that are considered "effectively nice." Where the Nice Guy Strategies sections provide insight on an individual level, Nice Company Strategies are introduced to provide prescriptive steps at an organizational level. In the Nice Company section, each strategy has several takeaways that show how these concepts can be assimilated into the workplace. We emphasize how managers and nonmanagers can simultaneously influence their companies to achieve more success and create a more positive work environment when these "nice" practices are applied. Providing guidance in both capacities will not only lead to developing more "effectively nice" guys but also to building "effectively nice" organizations.

## CHAPTER 1

YOU HAVE THE RIGHT TO:

# Self-Awareness

KNOW YOUR
STRENGTHS AND
WEAKNESSES

> "Ninety percent of the world's woe comes from people not knowing themselves, their abilities, their frailties, and even their real virtues. Most of us go almost all the way through life as complete strangers to ourselves."
> — *Sydney J. Harris, popular American journalist*

## NICE GUY SYNDROME
# The Challenge of Self-Awareness

Accoring to Immanuel Kant, the eighteenth-century German philosopher, "That man can be conscious of himself in his contemplation raises him infinitely above all other living creatures on Earth." Unfortunately, many overly nice guys don't have a high level of self-awareness, which hinders their ability to rise to higher levels of effectiveness and success. They lack proper consciousness of themselves, their thoughts, their behavior, and their actions. They're often in denial of their shortcomings as they go through their daily life—oblivious to how their choices (or lack thereof) are creating their lack of success.

Sticking one's head in the sand in denial is counterproductive and often quite destructive. Ignoring bad news doesn't make it go away. The bad news might temporarily be "out of sight, out of mind," but it rarely goes away and, if not addressed, will likely lead to bad consequences down the road.

## The Stories

The following two stories are based on real events and illustrate a few of the self-awareness challenges that nice guys face in the business world. These stories represent distinct situations but have some common themes: the first concerning serving others at work and the second in the context of professional networking.

Each story is intentionally left open-ended—without resolution. What would *you* do? Would you be self-aware in situations like these? How might you go about establishing more self-knowledge to enhance your effectiveness? Would you be able to commit to prioritizing self-awareness over the long haul? Would this self-knowledge increase in its clarity and value over time? It's not easy to possess the kind of candid self-awareness we need to deal constructively with our weaknesses as well as capitalize fully on our strengths. Yet, honest, penetrating self-awareness is foundational to learning, growing, and establishing balanced effectiveness throughout our careers.

### Overly Nice . . . Overly Committed

"I can't figure out why I am always so overcommitted," Ben was saying to a coworker. "I always seem to be way behind in my work." Ben, who worked for a customer service firm that offered support, training, and consultation to small businesses, was one of the nicest people you could ever meet. He seemed to be always running off to another event or task that he had agreed to in order to help others out. He also seemed perpetually stressed and rushing to complete projects. It was normal to catch him a little out of breath and arranging for last-minute details to be completed, whether for copies, handouts, or word processing of written reports.

One of the most troubling aspects of Ben's pattern of mindlessly overcommitting was that he was never able to keep up with his own projects—the ones that he originated or led. Arguably, this inconsistent progress on the projects he "owned" had delayed his career advancement. He was a middle-level manager in the firm, and his skills were clearly well developed. He had a wealth of experience. That is a large part of why so many colleagues came to him for help, and why he could never say no to anyone, despite having a full plate of commitments. Others saw what Ben could not. They were truly puzzled that Ben could not figure out why he was always behind in his own work. "I'm going to cut back on the number of things I commit to," Ben announced with authority one day. It really appeared that he meant it this time. Two days later he agreed to help out a coworker on a substantial project involving design and delivery of a pilot training program. After briefly lamenting his having to take three days out of his busy schedule to attend and support the core training event for this program, the phone rang. "I don't know. I'm awfully busy right now, Megan," Ben said hesitantly to the caller. "I see, that is going to be tough. I guess I can help you out. What do I need to do?"

### Standing in the Way

There were several hundred people spread throughout the large ballroom at the Breakthrough Technology conference reception. Trent was standing next to his friend Sanjay as part of a circle of six people in conversation. "So tell me more about that new project you're working on," Trent said to his friend as he turned to face Sanjay more directly. This surprised Sanjay since someone else in the circle was already talking. Trent didn't seem to notice as he slowly, unconsciously was turning his back to the circle, separating himself and Sanjay from the rest of the group. His full attention and interest were focused only on Sanjay.

This was a consistent pattern for Trent and one that he didn't seem to be aware of. In large gatherings, he was more comfortable singling out a close friend or colleague and filtering out everyone else. Trent wondered why he didn't have a wider circle of friends in his profession, but he never really took the time for personal reflection that might have provided some answers to this challenge area. He typically attended four or five conferences a year where he gathered with his peers for meetings, presentations, and workshops to exchange information and new ideas. Still, his network of colleagues and friends was surprisingly small. While information in his line of work was often proprietary, the relationships and networking often led to the kind of collaboration and exchange of information that was needed for innovation. Thus, having a significant network of friends and colleagues that he could rely upon was an important part of career success.

Sanjay turned to face the others in the circle to signal to Trent that he wished to remain in conversation with the whole group rather than in a one-on-one with him. Without realizing it, this caused Trent to turn his back to the circle and block Sanjay off from the others. Trent sensed that Sanjay was becoming uncomfortable. "Your project sounds really interesting," Trent said. "I would really like to know more about it." Trent made it clear that all his interest and attention were focused on Sanjay alone.

Meanwhile, to Sanjay's disappointment, the others were gradually re-forming to create a four-person circle as they continued their conversation about a new voice-recognition-technology process that was gaining momentum in their industry. The process sounded to Sanjay like it might be just the thing he needed to move his current project to the next stage. At that moment Sanjay made the decision not to invite Trent, as he had planned, to join him and some of his colleagues for dinner that evening.

## The Motives and Symptoms

Both of these situations point to the fundamental importance of nice guys having significant self-awareness in order to lay the foundation for greater effectiveness. In Ben's case, he was a really nice guy who sincerely wanted to help his colleagues and coworkers as much as he could. Consequently, he ended up helping everyone to such a degree that he sabotaged his ability to complete his own projects. His concern for others was so pronounced that he was becoming paralyzed in his primary work responsibilities and career.

Trent, on the other hand, valued his friends and wanted to give them his full attention but didn't realize that he was in fact smothering and cutting them, and himself, off from others. As a result he unintentionally pushed people away. In both cases nice people, driven by seemingly exemplary motives, overprioritized the needs of others. Ironically, this worked against them and diminished their ability to help others effectively.

Even the most well-intentioned motives can lead nice people to lose their effectiveness when they lack the awareness needed to act with balance. By overcommitting through automatic "yes" responses to requests, nice guys like Ben can defeat their own careers and become less valuable to their organizations. In Trent's case, by focusing on certain colleagues to the exclusion of others, not only is he missing out on the opportunities that can be gained from a large and healthy network, he is acting in a way that can handicap his closest colleagues as well. And all this largely occurs unintentionally because of a lack of self-awareness. This lack of self-awareness, which ultimately can lead nice people to be less effective and hinder their careers, is a foundational part of the Nice Guy Syndrome.

So what are the symptoms related to a lack of self-awareness? Three key symptoms are listed below:

1. *Self-Delusion.* For nice guys, this symptom can be particularly insidious and was apparent in both of the above examples. When people become overly focused on trying to be helpful and nice to others, an imbalance results, diminishing their effectiveness as colleagues. Even when evidence exists that suggests things are not going as well as they should, nice guys have a tendency to delude themselves into thinking that throwing even more niceness at the situation will eventually win the day. Sometimes they believe that placing their entire focus on others, even when it is apparent that it is not working, is the best course of action. They fall victim to an illogical, self-sabotaging belief that by being overly nice and helping everyone else—even to the detriment of their own careers—everything will work out in the end.

2. *Self-Denial.* Delusion becomes even more problematic when it triggers self-denial. Even when confronted with clear signals, overly nice guys often don't accept that they need to change. Instead they engage in self-denial, which can lead them to not only continue but to increase their ineffective behavior. When they have problems in their work, and it becomes clear that they are headed for even deeper troubles, they refuse to accept that they are the source of the difficulties. Something in their DNA leads them to deny the problem, and they continue to engage in their self-sabotaging behavior.

3. *Pattern "Unrecognition."* Overly nice guys have a difficult time recognizing that they are displaying clear self-defeating patterns. They may grasp the fact that something they are doing is diminishing their effectiveness, but lack the awareness that it's their own behavior that is the source of the problem. They simply don't recognize the connection between their behavior and the unintended consequences.

It's not unusual for the self-awareness gene to be absent in overly nice people. After all, they tend to focus on others and support them rather than focus on their own patterns of behavior and performance. Both of the cases mentioned above clearly reflect this outward focus. Yet, as is too often the case when less balanced extreme behavior is selected, even when it seems to be the "nice" thing to do, long-term outcomes tend to suffer. The good news is that there are effective nice guy strategies that can help.

## NICE GUY STRATEGIES
### Know Thyself

It's been said, "The truth shall set you free." For overly nice guys, this mainly applies to the truth about themselves. When it comes to self-awareness, they need to know the good, the bad, and the ugly, and they especially need to acknowledge areas where they are deluding themselves, in denial, or just falling short. That's because a clear awareness of our own (and our team's) strengths and weaknesses—along with an honest appraisal of current circumstances—helps create a solid foundation from which informed choices can be made. Overly nice guys must learn to take off the blinders and look at life with clarity and honesty.

In the words of Ernest Holmes, author of *The Science of Mind,* "It is through the revelation of the self, to the self, that one understands life." Confronting this truth and gaining this understanding, however, is challenging work and demands difficult choices. A conscious self-appraisal is required, which demands rigorous honesty—whether you're applying it to your own situation in particular or to the plight of your company in general. It is imperative that we learn to truly *know* ourselves. This process encourages overly nice guys to welcome constructive feedback, acknowledge their weaknesses without shame, nurture their strengths, and live by a strict code of integrity.

The payoff can be significant. Being honest about our own strengths and weaknesses encourages us to grow and make changes. As we become aware of our weaknesses, we can then find ways to effectively eliminate or offset them by seeking out training, mentoring, and/or people with complementary skills. Self-awareness also reduces the need to feel defensive, since we will be among the first to recognize valid criticism and necessary change.

### NICE GUY STRATEGY: Inventory

The first step on the road to self-awareness is to take a personal inventory. A retail store takes an inventory with the goal of making a list of *everything* that exists in the store at that time. In a similar way, a personal inventory takes stock to determine what exists on the "shelves" of one's life, job, and career. It's an honest appraisal of your abilities, habits, skills, and personal characteristics.

To start, make an accounting, in writing, of *all* of your strengths and weaknesses. In this book, we are focusing on how they relate to your work life and career (although you can certainly utilize this exercise to apply the same principles to your personal life). You must be thorough and honest or it will not be effective. Answering some of the following questions may help spur on a lively internal dialogue:

I'm happiest at work when I _____.
I'm really good at _____.
I do a great job when I get to _____.
It's really challenging at work for me to _____.
I really screwed up the last time I had to _____.

I tend to flounder when I'm asked to _____.

I regularly avoid _____ as I don't want to upset people.

If I mustered up the courage to speak on _____, the company would benefit by _____.

According to legendary U.S. Supreme Court justice Louis Brandeis, "Sunlight is said to be the best of disinfectants." Brandeis was speaking of the power of "light" (i.e., awareness) to "disinfect" (i.e., remove falsehood and reveal truth). In Brandeis's case, he was directly referring to the power of the courts, law, and the media to ferret out crime and corruption. In the case of overly nice guys, they must be willing to shine the light of truth upon their dark areas and ferret out hidden problems and deficiencies. Are you too nice a guy? Do you let other people take advantage of your good nature? Do you let other people treat you like a doormat and walk all over you? Do you struggle with speaking up, setting boundaries, confronting others, or holding people accountable?

In business, a commitment to self-awareness is a crucial skill. It's important to break the pattern of denial and delusion that leads overly nice guys to ignore problems and hope they'll go away. Make the commitment to acknowledge and strengthen the areas where growth is needed. John Pepper, formerly the CEO of Procter & Gamble and currently the chairman of the Disney Corporation, says that when hiring people he looks for such qualities, including "elements of integrity, of courage, of being willing to take on a tough issue and deal with it directly rather than hope it will cure itself."

It's okay to admit your fears and "failures." In fact, it's *healthy*. Once they are identified, it's much easier to get beyond them. Everyone has weaknesses. No one can excel at everything. What you might call a weakness is merely an area where you have room for personal growth or where there are skills that you need to acquire. The inventory process might also reveal that your current job is not a good fit for you. Not everyone is good at accounting, so everyone need not be an accountant! But you may need training to gain modest budgeting skills so that you can be a competent manager.

While doing your self-assessment, it can be extremely helpful to get "external views" (i.e., feedback from other people at work whom you trust). Jon Luther of Dunkin' Brands knows the importance of self-awareness and getting input from others. "You always need someone to look at you," he says. "Seeking advice is a signal of strength, not a sign of weakness. If they're honest with you, other people help give you more awareness of areas where you need to improve." To receive a well-rounded assessment, he suggests getting feedback from people who are vested in your success as well as from people who are *not* vested.

Be mindful when choosing the people you're asking for input. Avoid anyone you cannot trust to be compassionate, considerate, supportive, and completely honest. Seek out people who support your goals and ambitions—people who can offer wisdom and insight that will help you reach them.

It's desirable to cultivate this dynamic of openness, honesty, trust, and feedback with your coworkers. Good communication is essential. "To me," says Herb Kelleher of Southwest Airlines, "'nice' means keeping people abreast of the progress—or lack of progress—that they're making so they're always aware of your opinion of their weaknesses and their strengths. That's the only way people can convert weaknesses into strengths. They have to know about it."

Once you've made your assessment, what do you do with it? As Albert Einstein said, "The definition of insanity is doing the same thing over and over again and expecting different results." What are the things that you do "over and over again" that are not serving you anymore? Try to identify them. They may be triggers, patterns, or self-defeating behaviors. Some essential questions:

What is having a negative impact on your work life and holding you back? What needs to change? What is needed to remove the obstacles in your path?

Take the answers and distill them down to the three or four most significant areas where you have room for professional growth. Then, with a boss or a trusted colleague, spend some time brainstorming ways to strengthen these areas. Think of ways to change the way you do things. Develop new patterns and behaviors that will move you in the right direction. Will education or training help you gain valuable new skills and knowledge? Would a business coach or mentor be helpful? Or perhaps a career shift would help, moving into a new job that plays to your strength and minimizes your weaknesses?

The following story tells of an executive director who received an external view from his board that he had a problem—he was "too nice a guy." While it stung to learn that it was affecting his performance, he didn't let it defeat him. Instead, he learned from the information and used it as an opportunity for significant growth.

### The Shift

Michael was executive director of the American Heart Association of Vermont. During the initial stages of his tenure, he got rave reviews of his performance from his board of directors, except for one area. In the words of the board president: "The problem is, Michael, you're too nice a guy." They were concerned that his "nice-guyness" was getting in the way of his being assertive and making tough decisions.

At first, Michael was defensive. "It was a blind spot for me—an area where others could see a deficiency that I just couldn't see," he said. He knew he needed to be more self-aware and clear up that blind spot.

"It was time to make a significant shift in my life and step up my leadership skills," remembered Michael. "I took it as an opportunity to embark on a journey of what it would look like to be a different kind of leader." Before the shift could happen, he had to take stock. What was his "default" mode? He realized that part of his identity was being liked. What had to change? He had to admit that people sometimes took advantage of his kindness, empathy, and compassion, and that sometimes he distanced himself from tough personnel decisions.

For example, one of his employees—while talented—consistently caused problems in the office with her truancy and general surliness. It was a problem, in spite of the fact that he'd given her feedback on her behavior and encouraged her to improve her work habits. And truth be told, Michael admitted, "I really hadn't made her accountable. There had yet to be any ramifications for her actions."

Michael realized that the way he was handling it wasn't doing anybody any favors. As part of his new awareness, he was committed to finding a new way to manage—a way that would incorporate the "tougher" skills that he needed to add but that was still in alignment with his personal and professional values. "To be effective, I had to be willing to change my identity and make decisions that might not be popular but would be in the best interest of the organization. I had to learn to be more assertive and stand firm for what was best for the organization. But assertive does *not* equal autocratic. I resisted the notion that being 'strong' meant that I had to become a dictatorial Hun. There is no correlation between being a good leader and being a jerk."

As he met with the truant employee, Michael was assertive and firm as he set clear and fair expectations with her. Unfortunately, she wasn't able to live up to those expectations, so he eventually had to lay her off. He had to make the right decision for the institution as a whole and for the health of the office in particular.

Michael realized that he was putting too much emphasis on "being liked"—occasionally to the detriment of the team. He finally let go of trying to win the popularity contest and instead focused on making the right decisions for the organization while retaining his consideration and civility. He owed it to his team—and to himself—to have the right people in the right jobs and to ensure that everyone was in alignment with their corporate values.

Finding the balance of being "nice" and being "tough" can be challenging. Where do you draw the line? "It's an issue that I've wrestled with when dealing with employee performance issues," says John Pepper. "I've learned to drop back to the basic questions: What do I need to do to serve the fundamental needs of the institution? And am I doing whatever I need to do in a way that reflects respect for other people and fairness in the way that I treat them?"

In addition, Michael realized that the issue wasn't just how much rope he would give the surly, truant employee. He also had to be aware of the impact of that employee's behavior on the rest of the staff, as he had noticed that it was starting to cause frustration and even resentment with several coworkers. Pepper agrees that these are issues that must be considered in such circumstances. "What is right for the people who are reporting to that difficult person?" asks Pepper. "This is a critical question, because everybody grows by virtue of the people with whom they work. Confronting these issues is one of the most difficult things people have to do."

**NICE GUY STRATEGY: Optimize**

While it's important to identify your weaknesses to ensure that they don't subconsciously sabotage your career, it's even more important not to dwell on them (and let them defeat you) or give them too much influence (and allow them to define you).

A much more effective and powerful strategy is to leverage your personal assets and optimize your strengths. Choose your job and construct your career around doing the things that you *love* to do and at which you excel. Overly nice guys, because of their tendency to be excessively self-sacrificing, often get stuck in jobs that aren't in alignment with their talents and goals. But they lack the awareness, assertiveness, and temerity to break out of that trap and make a change. They fail to optimize their strengths.

This strategy is also relevant for those whom you manage. Put people in a position to be successful by placing them in jobs that optimize their talents and minimize their shortcomings. According to Jim Turley of Ernst & Young, "We have people who think that they have to do *everything*, and that means that too much of their time is spent in areas of weakness. Instead, let them do what they're great at."

People on your team are frequently not aware of their strengths and weaknesses, and telling them about their deficiencies can be extremely difficult. While managers at all levels must strive to optimize the effectiveness of their team (and sometimes their peers), giving feedback can be very difficult to do, and very painful to hear. Whether it's a subordinate, a colleague, a boss, or a business partner, if that person's area of weakness is affecting business, something must be said, as Frank learned in the following story.

### The End Game

For almost ten years, Frank and his two partners (Rhonda and Nigel) have had a thriving design firm, specializing in both advertising and Web design. Whenever a new job came through the door, whichever partner was available would take it on. That's the way it had always been done. As business increased, however, this way of distributing work was becoming less and less productive and effective. Frank and Rhonda realized that they needed to do an inventory of the firm's strengths and weaknesses—including an objective evaluation of each employee—to help them determine how they should reorganize to facilitate growth.

During this process, Frank and Rhonda both realized that evaluating their partner Nigel's talents would demand special attention. While Nigel excelled at advertising, it had become apparent to them that he struggled with Web design. It was becoming more and more of a hindrance to the firm's success and growth. To meet their goals, they both knew that a change had to be made. Somehow, they would have to shift Nigel away from Web design and toward a narrower focus on advertising.

"We weren't sure how Nigel would perceive a shift in his job description," said Frank. "We wanted to be nice. We wanted to avoid clubbing him over the head with a negative assessment. After all, Nigel was a founding partner and a close friend. If we confronted him and said that his Web design work wasn't cutting it, would he see it as a slap in the face? Would he see a shift in responsibilities as a demotion? He might even get upset and leave the firm. Given his value to the business, we really wanted to avoid this."

Frank and Rhonda decided to look at the problem differently. "What was the end game?" they asked each other. What was the larger goal to which they could all agree? The growth and success of the business was the end game. To achieve this goal, it was in the best interest of the company that everyone played to his or her strengths. Nigel's strength was advertising, and they wanted to optimize that strength by encouraging him to take charge of it. "We hoped to get him excited about growing this part of the business," Frank said. "We wanted to turn this into a positive. So

Rhonda and I worked together to make a pitch to Nigel that would position this shift as a positive for both him and the company. We framed it as a big *opportunity,* not a screwup."

After they made their pitch, they were relieved that Nigel gladly agreed to their solution. He relinquished all Web design work and enthusiastically took on his new responsibilities. "He almost seemed relieved," said Frank. "I'm not sure if he had admitted to himself that he was struggling with Web design, but as we all discussed future growth and possible changes, it became the obvious solution. It was a win-win for everybody."

If a corporate culture has failed to foster an environment where honest feedback is normal and expected, it can be difficult to "drop a bomb" on someone out of the blue, such as the situation with Nigel. Considering the circumstances, they did a great job of optimizing everyone's strengths and moving the issue to a successful outcome. However, if they had a company tradition of openly offering honest input and feedback, they would likely have had far less fear of hurting Nigel's feelings and possibly losing him over making an internal change in responsibilities. This is not to single out Frank, because his plight is *extremely* common in our culture. Giving and receiving honest feedback is one of *the* most difficult—and most important—things to do if you want to be highly effective and successful in business. But it is surprisingly rare because of our insatiable need to be "nice."

Joe McGuire of Tweeter says, "If you are not being straightforward and honest, you're actually not serving the person. That is just as dishonest as telling them a lie, because you're letting someone go along thinking that everything is all right—and it's not."

Jim Turley from Ernst & Young ran the firm's Minneapolis office for four years. As he prepared to move to New York, one of the people from the Minneapolis office said, "Jim, what you did better than others was you put us into roles in which we could succeed. We didn't always like it when you said, 'No, here is your role. You're Steve Kerr. You're not Michael Jordan.' You sometimes put us in a role that we may have thought wasn't right for us, but invariably we'd realize that they were roles that would capitalize on our individual strengths and didn't cause us to try to figure out how to hide our weaknesses every day."

To successfully optimize your strengths—and the strengths of others—defensiveness must be reduced or, better yet, alleviated. For overly nice guys, this can be quite difficult. As we've stated, a weakness is merely an area where there is room for personal growth. It is not a reason to feel humiliated, diminished, or defeated—or to get defensive and attack the person who is offering the well-intended input.

Here are a few techniques that can help reduce the tendency to be defensive:

1. *Wear Your Armor.* Don't be thin-skinned. Allow critical comments to bounce off you by wearing "armor" that protects *you*—and your self-esteem—from your *work* that is being evaluated (and criticized). It's very important to separate yourself from your work as best as you can and take an objective stance. Do not take the comments of others as a personal attack. Take the emotion and judgment out of the equation by "getting to neutral" and viewing the comment in an impartial and open-minded way.

2. *Selective Memory.* Don't let the criticism and mistakes get you down and stay with you for a long period of time. Overly nice guys can choose to have a "short memory" by quickly moving past a difficult incident and focusing on the next task at hand.

3. *Think Before You React.* When someone makes a less than flattering comment about your work, resist the urge to get defensive and lash back with an inappropriate remark. Instead of a productive conversation, it can quickly degenerate into a battle of egos. Make sure your brain is in gear before engaging your mouth!

**NICE GUY STRATEGY: Intention**

You've taken your personal inventory and identified three key areas that need attention. You've learned that it's best to optimize your strengths—spending your time and energy doing the things at which you excel. The final strategy for self-awareness is to live with intention. In the words of the writer Henry David Thoreau, "If one advances confidently in the direction of one's dreams, and endeavors to live the life which one has imagined, one will meet with a success unexpected in common hours."

"To live the life which one has imagined," Thoreau said. Have *you* taken the time to imagine the life and career that you want . . . with clear intention? If you haven't, you're living by default—a common problem for overly nice guys. When you live by default, things often seem to randomly "happen" to you in your life—which likely leaves you feeling frustrated, unlucky, and victimized by circumstances. Baseball legend Yogi Berra said it best: "If you don't know where you're going, you'll end up someplace else."

It's important to shift this perception of life. Start living with intention. Overly nice guys need to sharpen their awareness and make their intentions known—to themselves and to the world. What do you *intend* to accomplish at work this week? What do you *intend* to experience in your career this year? How do you *intend* for your business to grow? Dr. Napoleon Hill, the author of the classic *Think and Grow Rich*, said, "Whatever the mind can conceive and believe, the mind can achieve." Hold your intentions in your mind, write them down, visualize them in your head, and then imagine them actually happening and becoming real. Then develop the practice of rewriting your intentions every morning, *knowing* that this is what you are attracting to your life. Know that this is the career that you are creating.

Once you put your intentions "out there," the wheels are in motion. "Announcing your interest is part of getting the job," says Doug Walker of REI. Opportunities will arise. Ideas will pop into your mind as you're watching TV, reading a magazine, or talking with a colleague. You'll begin meeting people who, in some way, shape, or form, can help you reach your goals. You'll begin to speak up at meetings, notice things that you didn't notice before, and seize new opportunities. It all starts with setting intentions and making conscious decisions about what you want. In the following story, Rob, a successful businessman, used the skill of intention setting to grow his business.

### The Road Map

When Rob became a small-business owner thirteen years ago, he realized he would need to change his modus operandi if he wanted to achieve the high level of success he desired. While reading books by business gurus such as Donald Trump, Wayne Dyer, and Zig Zigler, Rob said, "I realized that intention setting was a common attribute that successful people shared. So I drank the Kool-Aid and became a disciple of setting goals and intentions. It's really powerful. It works."

Rob sets annual goals every January and then reviews them on a quarterly basis. He equates it to "planting a seed" or "setting an intention that keeps revealing the path that will get you to where you want to go—like a road map. Yes, you need to review them periodically, but I find they also become a subliminal part of my daily life. When you set an intention, you open yourself up to every thing that it takes to accomplish it."

He is quick to differentiate between tasks and goals. A task is a *have* to do, whereas a goal is a *want* to do. He *has* to get groceries, fill up his gas tank, call a client, and pay his taxes. He *wants* to own a new home, pay down his debt, build a prosperous business, and enter a new vertical market. His goals and intentions move him toward his dreams and desires.

For Rob, intentions are also a prioritization tool. "When I set an intention, I've made the decision that it is important to me," he said. "It effectively becomes a working strategy." Every time he reviews them, it brings him back to center and consciously reminds him of where he's going and what he's creating. "It also stretches you," he added. "You're really putting yourself out there. And it humbles you, too. You have to be willing to risk *not* reaching your goal and be honest with yourself, admit it, readjust, and then you can go after it again."

"Luck is the residue of design," according to Branch Rickey, general manager of the Brooklyn Dodgers in the 1950s. When you set intentions, you are essentially designing your day and your life. The more intentional you are, the more you create opportunities to be "lucky."

Overly nice guys can give their intentions added energy and strength by writing a personal vision statement that reflects the goals that they've set and their new vision for their job, their career, and their life. You can take it further and create your own personal manifesto, where you declare (in document form) your intentions. You can do this same exercise with your team and your organization, creating a common vision for the future of the business.

## NICE GUY WHIPLASH: Self-Awareness

When an overly nice guy overdoes it with self-awareness and goes too far in the other direction, it can cause problems. It can cause a Nice Guy Whiplash that may take one or more of the following forms:

1. *Self-Flagellation.* While going through a self-assessment, some overly nice guys focus too much on their weaknesses and

become extremely harsh and self-critical. Becoming obsessed with (or even ashamed of) these perceived shortcomings is self-defeating and can cripple their ability to function in a productive way.

2. *Navel-Gazing.* Overindulging in the process of self-awareness sometimes creates self-absorbed people who are out of touch with the realities of the business world. Their obsessive focus on their own thoughts and feelings can cause them to lose sight of basic goals and objectives. Time and energy is wasted as they allow themselves to get mired in process and nuance.

## NICE COMPANY STRATEGIES
# Controls for Self-Awareness

Most organizations employ some type of "control" to ensure that a process, product, or person is performing as expected. For financial reporting in the United States, the Sarbanes-Oxley Act of 2002 was introduced with a specific emphasis on implementing financial controls in response to a number of corporate and accounting scandals. The International Organization for Standardization established ISO 9000 to introduce controls for the manufacturing of products. For people, an assortment of controls can be employed such as job descriptions and employee evaluations (albeit without the formality of a governing body that defines specific standards).

What type of controls can be established to help overly nice guys in your company develop more self-awareness? How can they help your business? When employers help overly nice guys

**JOE MCGUIRE**
**FORMER CEO, TWEETER HOME ENTERTAINMENT GROUP**

People, if they're at all self-actualizing, should have the ability to continue to grow, learn, and develop.

increase their self-awareness, they will overcome many of the
symptoms associated with Nice Guy Syndrome. Business will benefit greatly as they develop a better understanding of their strengths
and weaknesses and then subsequently learn to optimize their
strengths. They become more balanced as they move from *overly*
nice to *effectively* nice. Your organization will reap many benefits
from this transformation.

We believe you *can* teach an old dog new tricks. Joe McGuire
of Tweeter shares, "People, if they're at all self-actualizing, should
have the ability to continue to grow, learn, and develop." Sam
DiPiazza of PricewaterhouseCoopers agrees and says, "The majority
of human behavior is taught throughout life. The experiencing of
life events can alter one's perspective."

Overly nice guys are typically willing and eager to learn how
they can improve. With guidance, they can become more self-
aware—which helps them to be more effective for themselves and
for your organization.


**NICE COMPANY STRATEGY: Inventory Controls**

Employees thrive in a corporate culture that is authentic. They
prefer to work for a company they can trust, one that is supportive
of people, and one that stays in alignment with the mission of the
organization. Dr. John Seffrin of the American Cancer Society
also believes it's important to "create an atmosphere where people
don't unduly worry about reprisals." For overly nice guys, if there
is an absence of trust and authenticity at work, it can be debilitating. If work isn't a safe place to be open, honest, and real, then
it's not a safe place to develop true self-awareness. In an unsafe
environment, they will feel suspicious and paranoid, worried
that any "weakness" they expose will be used against them. But if
the culture has high integrity and authenticity, it will attract

employees who are willing to be honest, courageous, forthright, and accountable.

Employing one or more of the following "controls" will help employees gain a better sense of self-awareness and breed a more authentic work environment:

1. *Feedback Controls.* Obtaining authentic feedback from your peers, managers, customers, and subordinates is challenging, especially for the overly nice guys who are afraid to give and receive it. What gets in the way is that people often perceive constructive feedback as negative and hurtful. They don't want to potentially damage someone's career (and their ego). Ironically, it's the *absence* of authentic feedback that is actually much more damaging to one's career. To address this, introduce a Feedback Control to indicate if people are providing authentic feedback when evaluating others. If the Feedback Control is low, this means that the person is not providing honest feedback to others during a review process. If it is high, this means that the person is authentic and providing insightful feedback. The Feedback Control can have a substantial impact on one's review, so care must be taken as to who should provide that input. It should directly impact both the person giving *and* the person receiving the review in a way that is consistent with your organization's incentive programs (financial, recognition, advancement, etc.). This ensures that people are authentic in their appraisals of others. At first, a Feedback Control may be a bit tricky to implement; however, when coupled with the right culture, it becomes a natural fit and a powerful tool.

2. *Focus Controls.* Overly nice guys often need guidance to keep them focused on areas of competency. Their enthusiasm and generosity can easily lead them to spend too much time on well-meaning but misguided endeavors, likely in an effort to help coworkers with projects and tasks that are well outside the overly nice guys' areas of expertise. A Focus Control can define and

measure how well they are consciously focusing on their areas of strength. And for managers who are responsible for building a team, a Focus Control can show how well they are counterbalancing their strengths (and the team's strengths) by hiring into their weaknesses and effectively counterbalancing them.

**JEFF TAYLOR**
**FOUNDER AND FORMER CEO,**
**MONSTER.COM;**
**FOUNDER AND CEO,**
**EONS.COM**

Hire into and balance your areas of weakness.

Focus Controls can aid overly nice guys and their counterparts in developing a higher level of self-awareness as they recognize the strengths and weaknesses of themselves and others. When Jeff Taylor of Monster.com was starting the business, he had no choice but to do most of the work himself. As he developed a higher level of self-awareness, he hired people to effectively counterbalance his weaknesses. He relinquished control over areas such as operations and finance to new C-level executives while preserving marketing and sales under his domain. This choice to focus on his strengths and hire into his weaknesses helped propel the company to a much higher level of growth and profitability. He also learned that if you forget to cultivate strong people below you within your areas of strength, you run the risk of creating a vacuum when your time eventually comes to give up control of that area.

Tess Mateo, PricewaterhouseCoopers' director, office of the CEO, works closely with CEO Sam DiPiazza. She agrees with Taylor's perspective. Mateo believes that "it is critical to have a 'wingman' to counterbalance the weaknesses of the person you are with. Mateo adds that "all parties involved have the appropriate level of self-awareness to determine those strengths and weaknesses." Doing so encourages honesty and creates balance, which ultimately leads to more productive teams and a more successful organization.

3. *Checkpoint Controls.* Most organizations perform annual reviews to provide feedback for their employees. However, due to the infrequency of performance reviews, they rarely address the need for immediate feedback. For this reason, Checkpoint Controls should be considered.

Checkpoint Controls are a brief set of three to five questions that capture the essence of your employee's performance as it applies to a given task or assignment. The challenge with Checkpoint Controls is to keep it short, to keep it meaningful, and to keep it authentic. If it is too lengthy, it becomes cumbersome and employees either rush through it or are reluctant to embrace it—thus negating its value.

**JIM TURLEY**
**CEO, ERNST & YOUNG**

The People Point is a very basic scale without any numeric values, and because of its brevity, its impact is immediately felt.

With regularity and authenticity, Checkpoint Controls can help overly nice guys gain immediate insight and quickly take corrective actions.

Jim Turley of Ernst & Young recognized the importance of immediacy and simplicity as they looked to augment their review process for 130,000 professionals around the globe. While the firm has historically used a variety of 360-degree feedback techniques, the unwieldiness of this method became overbearing. As a result, Ernst & Young introduced a supplemental technique called "The People Point," which summarizes overall performance with one simple measure. "The People Point is a very basic scale without any numeric values," shares Turley, "and because of its brevity, its impact is immediately felt." In this process, an evaluator picks a point on the line to denote "how well the person is supporting the people, culture, and values of the firm"—with a range from low to high. The People Point was well received and enthusiastically implemented. While additional techniques are also implemented to supplement and expand upon the People Point, Turley likes the way it directly drives a higher level of awareness.

Individually or collectively, these Inventory Controls allow overly nice guys in your organization to develop their self-awareness in a more meaningful and timely fashion. In the context of self-awareness, it is important to point out that a "control" is not intended to be as structured as Sarbanes-Oxley or ISO 9000 controls. The use of the term "control" is to provide meaningful guidelines. The guidelines for your nice guys are such that they can develop a higher degree of self-awareness to be more effective.

### NICE COMPANY STRATEGY: War Stories

Through the telling of War Stories, companies illustrate positive and negative outcomes—often with a fun or interesting twist. People can live vicariously through stories, learn from the past, and bond in the shared experience of past successes and failures. The group examines the stories together and—with good support and humor—helps members understand what was done effectively and ineffectively.

Quinn, a marketing director for a motorcycle manufacturing company, is a fan of War Stories. He brings his internal and external PR team together on a quarterly basis. With a deliberate emphasis on informality, Quinn turns it into a social function by bringing in ice cream to "melt" any barriers to open and honest discussion. They generally talk about what went right, what went wrong, what was fun, what was painful, and how they'd do it the next time.

One of the questions regularly asked by Quinn is if there were any occurrences of Nice Guy Syndrome in their stories—regardless of whether it was a staff member, a PR agency representative, or a media outlet contact. People typically share their thoughts about Syndrome issues along with steps that can be taken to avoid recurrences. Quinn's techniques have worked well as he and his team enjoy a comfortable, open environment that allows for the free exchange of ideas. This activity has provided a great mechanism for people to learn from one another without the structure (and implications) of a formal review process.

In support of the War Stories strategy, here are a few techniques that can be utilized to provide guidance and structure while ensuring that they stay on track:

1. *Preselect Storytellers.* It is recommended that you identify a few stories and storytellers prior to partaking of a War Story session. This eliminates any initial awkwardness that may be associated with people volunteering to tell their stories. Alternately, an experienced War Story culture may support more of an ad hoc experience where employees spontaneously jump in with their respective stories.

2. *War Story Facilitation.* It is recommended that a seasoned leader facilitate the War Story process. This person can guide the discussion in a positive and productive direction while ensuring that the environment stays relaxed and conducive to good dialogue.

3. *Group Size.* It may be appropriate to break a larger group into smaller groups, with each group concentrating on the analysis of one story. Alternatively, the entire group can review multiple stories with an understanding that bigger groups may inhibit some people from speaking up authentically, especially overly nice guys who are shy and introverted.

Throughout the War Story process, it is important to stress that a high level of comfort and trust must exist among the group, with the understanding that stories can be shared without fear of retribution. Additionally, it should be very clear as to the level of knowledge or expertise people should have prior to participating in a War Story session.

## Chapter Summary

### NICE GUY MOTIVES AND SYMPTOMS

**Self-Delusion** Overly nice guys have a tendency to delude themselves into thinking that throwing even more niceness at the situation will eventually win the day.

**Self-Denial** Self-denial often follows self-delusion as ineffective behavior continues. In this capacity, overly nice guys refuse to accept the difficult situations they create for themselves.

**Pattern "Unrecognition"** When people lack the self-awareness to detect their repeated patterns of being overly nice, they experience the Pattern "Unrecognition" symptom.

### NICE GUY STRATEGIES

**Inventory** Overly nice guys must take a personal inventory to determine what exists on the "shelves" of their work life. It's an honest appraisal of their abilities, habits, skills, and personal characteristics.

**Optimize** For overly nice guys, it's best for them to leverage and optimize their personal assets and play to their strengths, and, in doing so, be mindful of their liabilities.

**Intentions** Create a vision and set goals to manifest the life that you want. If you haven't, you're living by default—a common problem for overly nice guys where things often seem to randomly "happen." Define your intentions and pursue them vigorously.

## NICE COMPANY STRATEGIES

**Inventory Controls**   Incorporate practical guidelines or controls into your evaluation programs to allow overly nice guys in your company to develop higher levels of self-awareness. These include practices to ensure that review feedback is authentic, that your team members are focused on their strengths and weaknesses, and that evaluations can be real-time and brief.

**War Stories**   Gather people together to share business (and personal) stories in meaningful ways. Let them see that everyone makes mistakes and then identify how they can learn from them.

## CHAPTER 2

YOU HAVE THE RIGHT TO:

# Speak Up

> LEARN TO EXPRESS
> YOUR OPINIONS
> AND BE HEARD

"The difference between the *almost*-right word and
the *right* word is really a large matter—it's the difference between
the lightning bug and lightning."
—*Mark Twain*

## NICE GUY SYNDROME

# To Speak or Not to Speak?

To speak or not to speak? That is the first of many questions for nice guys in business. *When* to speak, to *whom* to speak, *what* to say, and *how* to say it are a few of the other questions that often come into play. Combined, they often make the seemingly simple act of putting thoughts into words feel like negotiating a verbal minefield.

Overly nice guys often prefer to remain silent rather than state their personal and managerial views or needs. They do so for a host of reasons, including the fear of being judged, the maintenance of the well-being of others, or the struggle with feelings of self-worth. In choosing silence, however, they are likely going to miss out on opportunities, advancement, and rewards that come to those who bring their thoughts and ideas forward.

## The Stories

The following two stories illustrate a few of the speak-up challenges that nice guys face in the business world: the first from a man who worked in sales for a lighting company, and the second from an officer in the navy.

Each story is intentionally left open-ended—without resolution. What would *you* do? Would you speak up? What would you say? To whom would you speak? Why? It's not always easy to discern what is "right" or "wrong," and the ramifications of speaking up (or not speaking up) can be significant—not only for the nice guy but also for those who are influenced and affected by the nice guy's behavior and choices.

### Amway or the Highway

Donald, a respected engineer, was Rick's co-manager and a consistent contributor to the success of their sales department at a lighting distributor. Since financial bonuses were pooled, it was important that the team always perform at its peak. Rick respected Donald but became concerned when he began overhearing phone conversations that clearly did not relate to business.

"Initially, I ignored the calls. Donald pulled his weight in sales and contributed to a positive work atmosphere. As the extracurricular phone traffic increased, however, I approached him about it. Without apologizing for the calls, he explained that he was involved in Amway—the largest multilevel marketing organization in the world. He offered me the opportunity to join him and invited me to attend a meeting. In the course of this conversation, Donald also explained that his commitment to Amway wasn't interfering with his performance at our company. Actually, he boasted that it helped motivate him to be a better team player. Since I hadn't noticed a falloff in his performance and since he seemed passionate about his new interest, I decided to give him the benefit of the doubt. I even attended a meeting as his guest. While I was not persuaded to join Amway, I decided to let the issue lie.

"A short time later, though, I was approached by Bob, a vendor who serviced our supply house. He told me nervously that he needed my advice and described how Donald was recruiting him to join 'the business opportunity of a lifetime!' Bob was torn: he didn't want to risk his relationship with Donald—sales might depend on it—by declining the invitation. What did I think he should do?

"I was mortified that Donald had, for his Amway commitment, violated basic business etiquette and company policy. I began to wonder how many other vendors—or even customers—Donald had put in the same awkward position."

### Green Card

Ray was an ensign in the navy, fresh out of the Academy and Surface Warfare Office Training School. During his time in the navy he worked with people of varying ranks. One of those people included a seaman recruit named Chan, who recently emigrated from the Philippines to the United States and was in the process of obtaining his green card for permanent residence. While completing the long process associated with obtaining the green card, Chan had relocated his family to the States and was understandably anxious that his application succeeded.

Unfortunately, Ray soon realized that the quality of Chan's work was inconsistent and that Chan lacked commitment. He often didn't complete his assignments properly and seemed unaware of any complications, despite the subtle hints that Ray was giving him. Casual discussions with Chan didn't seem to make much difference in his conduct or effectiveness. Ray knew that Chan's performance was putting a number of projects in jeopardy, but he hesitated to take any action, at least in part because of Chan's personal situation.

There are perfectly good reasons to "be nice" and choose to remain silent in these situations. In Rick's case, he feels loyalty to a member of his team who has been a strong performer. He could choose to avoid addressing Donald's extracurricular business interests because Donald still contributes effectively to the team. Ray exhibits a strong concern for the professional and personal well-being of others. He recognizes the enormous cost to Chan if he loses his job—a cost not just to his employment but also to his family's stability and long-range plans.

As motives go, these are all excellent reasons not to speak up. They explain why many of us consider ourselves nice guys and like to be considered as such by others. We're fair, tolerant, compassionate, and willing to go the extra mile for a friend or colleague. But we also know that these qualities can represent—and result in—ineffectual management, with very real consequences for us and for our organizations. This behavior ultimately results in a lack of effectiveness, leadership, and long-term success—i.e., the Nice Guy Syndrome.

What are the symptoms of the Nice Guy Syndrome as related to speaking up? They are expressed through various acts, emotions, and behaviors.

1. *Fear of Being Judged.* Overly nice guys, either consciously or unconsciously, tend to fear acting with decisive judgment. They often harbor concerns about how their colleagues will perceive managerial actions that they might take. They wonder whether speaking up will make them look foolish or cause others to be angry with them.

2. *Sense of Unworthiness.* Nice guys struggle with issues of ego and worthiness. They are often unsure about the validity of their managerial judgment and the value of their opinion. They wrestle with concerns about upsetting or even inflicting havoc on others if they speak.

3. *Lack of Confidence in Speaking Ability.* Nice guys sometimes question their ability to speak in appropriate ways. Not being confident that they will say the right thing, they often believe their best option is to simply remain silent. Finding the right strategy for saying what needs to be said—and the words to deliver a particular message—can be harder than saying nothing at all. This is especially true for nice guys who are not sure of themselves. However, silence can communicate tactlessness in the same way the wrong words can. Saying nothing can be seen as a lack of faith in the receiving party's ability to listen, understand, and/or respond appropriately.

4. *Inability to Really Listen.* One of the most challenging skills to learn in life is how to listen. It's quite common to hear without really listening. Or perhaps we hear what we *want* to hear instead of what is actually being said. Overly nice guys often struggle with this challenge. When they are concerned about how they are coming across, and whether they are causing problems for or being judged by others, they can get caught up in mentally framing a reply without really hearing what is being said.

Learning to speak up effectively is one of the most challenging things for nice people to learn. Rick and Ray both struggled with this challenge. And their stories suggest symptoms related to a fear of being judged, a sense of unworthiness, a fear of saying the wrong thing, and a lack of ability to really listen. Many of us have seen similar behaviors in our colleagues and ourselves. They are the downside to being an overly nice guy. Until we address these tendencies within ourselves and develop the capacity to speak up when we need to, we will be vulnerable to the Nice Guy Syndrome.

## NICE GUY STRATEGIES
# What I Say

The ability to articulate our thoughts—to speak up—is fundamental to business success. Unfortunately, it frequently is one of
the overly nice guy's greatest challenges. Situations that necessitate expressing opinions to others—to an audience of one (a boss,
for instance) or many (at a large event)—can be very intimidating.

Some people are able to summon the courage needed to speak
up, while others shrink from the challenge. Is this type of courage
something that can be learned? Can it be institutionalized and
integrated into a corporate culture? Can these problems be overcome?

We say yes to all of these questions. If you aim to be successful,
you must step up and do what's needed. Here are three key strategies that will help you do so.

### NICE GUY STRATEGY: Prepare

An informed viewpoint is worth infinitely more than an igno-
rant one. Preparation breeds confidence—confidence that will be
apparent when you speak to others. Rudy Giuliani, who started
as a lawyer and U.S. district attorney before becoming mayor of
New York City and a 2008 presidential candidate, said his first
boss told him to "spend four hours preparing for every one hour
in court."

As part of your preparation, it's helpful to develop a strategy
that first determines which audience to target and then defines
how best to address it—whether you're making a cold call on the
phone, approaching a celebrity keynote speaker after his or her
speech, speaking with your boss about a difficult issue, working

the room at a business cocktail party, raising a new idea at a staff meeting, or confronting a customer with a pressing concern. Speaking off the cuff, or "winging it," rarely leads to concise, effective communication. Instead, set a clear intention for the conversation and prepare a thoughtful line of questioning that reflects that intention.

The following story speaks to the importance of preparation in achieving a desired outcome when speaking up.

### Doing Away with SWAG

Alan, a VP of development at a West Coast college, learned the hard way that "SWAG" (Scientific Wild-Ass Guesses) would not help him get the raise he wanted.

"I've worked for Bob, the college president, for more than five years," he said, "and I've realized that you need to speak up or you'll get run over. Bob loves to debate. It's his nature and it always made it difficult for me to speak up on issues —especially when it came to my salary review. In the past, I tried to cover the subject of compensation but never had much success. He always argued with me, and he always won.

"This year I tried something different," he continued. "I decided to do extensive research on my salary compared to others at institutions similar to mine." Alan used a strategic plan to get a list of their top competitors and then got salary information about his position at these institutions. He also used a human resources benchmark for other comparable institutions.

"I walked into the review armed and dangerous," he remembered. "Guess what happened. When I shared the information at the appropriate time in the meeting, Bob was stunned. I was so prepared with good information, it completely caught him off guard. He couldn't argue with the facts. Speaking up is *much* easier when you're prepared. It breeds confidence. Good research and preparation equals good results. In my next check, it paid off handsomely."

After several failures, Alan finally realized that he needed to do a better job of speaking his boss's language. Because he did his homework, prepared thoroughly, knew the material, and got his facts straight, he was standing on solid ground during his salary negotiation. Bob sensed it and ultimately offered his respect, attention, and a raise in return.

## NICE GUY STRATEGY: Calibrate

We see the world through our own filters—filters that are informed by our unique set of experiences, ideas, and values. This perception of the world creates our own personal reality. It's natural. We're human. But here's the rub: invariably, we tend to expect everyone else to think, feel, speak, act, and respond the way that we do. When they don't, we are shocked. What is *wrong* with them? Why did they *say* that? Why didn't they do it *my* way? It's because everyone has his or her *own* filters, perceptions, and subjective reality.

Gifted communicators understand this concept at a deep level. They do not expect others to be exactly like them. Instead, they aim to think like their target audience. They put themselves in other people's shoes and strive to understand their perspectives, motivations, and desires. "Tuning in" to the mood of specific individuals, the tenor of a given situation, and the specifics of the environment generates invaluable information that can inform the way you speak.

Be flexible and creative. What approach will be most effective in this moment? Humor? Boldness? Deference? Should you make a serious statement or tell a whimsical story? Be aware of all relevant factors and calibrate your approach accordingly. If your audience feels understood, respected, and engaged in an appropriate way, your chances of success increase dramatically.

Sloppy calibration, on the other hand, often leads to misdirected communication, frustration, and even anger. Has a scolding by your boss in the morning ever caused you to speak inappropriately and lash out at one of your peers or employees in the afternoon? If you "miss the target" and don't speak directly to the source of your frustration, your anger is likely to seep out in a stream of petty, misdirected complaints and resentments that can be destructive and disrespectful toward others.

Another key component of effective calibration is active listening. Speaking up is one thing, but if you're not fully engaged with your audience as they speak—and responding in appropriate ways—then your words are diminished and you'll likely fail in your mission to be effective and, ultimately, successful. Strive to remain flexible, and avoid mindlessly adhering to your own agenda without considering and respecting your audience.

In the following story, Jay had to calibrate his comments carefully and be mindful of how and when he spoke his mind . . . or risk being made irrelevant.

### Save Your Bullets

Jay has worked at a large governmental space agency for more than twenty years. He has been a lead space flight program engineer, manager of advanced technologies, and the PR man who speaks at schools about future Mars missions. While it's *not* hard to keep your job at a government agency, it *is* challenging to remain effective and relevant. He must carefully calibrate his words and actions on an ongoing basis.

Jay described his experience as follows:

"There's an expression to 'save your bullets,' meaning you've got maybe six silver bullets in your career and must use them wisely and tactfully. You do not want to be labeled as a 'complainer.' Next thing you know, you are not invited to meetings anymore.

"There are many times when keeping your mouth shut is the best approach—mostly if the impact of the organization taking what you believe is the 'wrong' course of action just doesn't matter *that* much.

"But if the impact of the wrong course of action *does* cross the line of being important, *definitely* speak up. 'Important' means (1) the safety of personnel, (2) mission success where failure will cost significant money, or (3) someone I like is at risk of losing credibility, etc. If the boss says no, you'd better have a *real* good reason to go to *his* boss, let alone your boss's boss's boss.

"I find it's helpful to find a 'first follower.' Meet with someone before the meeting and ask him or her to back you up during a touchy discussion. Or during the meeting, be a good observer of who might be nodding in agreement and ask them directly what they think about what you said."

Jay learned how to calibrate his approach based on each situation in particular and the agency's culture in general. This skill is crucial if he wishes to remain effective in the agency for the long haul. Bill Allen of Outback Steakhouse knows the importance of good calibration. "One needs to employ the appropriate level of tact and finesse when participating in meetings—be it a board presentation or a general meeting. Most of the time, it is best to express concerns with someone privately—*after* a group meeting. However, publicly speaking up in these situations is critical when a course of action is proposed that is fundamentally wrong. This is when tact, finesse, and discernment become very important as people gauge the intensity of your message and react accordingly."

## NICE GUY STRATEGY: Engage

You've done your preparation thoroughly, and then you thoughtfully calibrated your intended communication. Now it's time to show up and participate. It's time to engage. Is your opinion valid? Given your research, experience, and expertise . . . absolutely! So put it out there. Engage the appropriate audience. You can't win if you don't play. What have you really got to lose by taking a chance and speaking up? Better still, what do you and your company have to *gain*?

If you don't engage, there can be a high price to pay—to you, to your company, and perhaps to your customers as well. "To me, it's very much about having the courage, frankly, to have difficult conversations," says Jim Turley of Ernst & Young. "For instance, if you're in the manufacturing of helicopters and someone is being too nice when they see a potential product defect—a defect that one of their colleagues or bosses or someone else had responsibility for—and they are noncombative, don't want to cause confrontation, and don't want to offend the other person . . . and they keep their mouth shut, you could have helicopters falling out of the sky."

You certainly won't be heard if you're a wallflower and hide in the back of the room—or, worse, if you play the doormat and let others take advantage of your good nature by offloading their problems and responsibilities onto you. "I'm an introvert," you protest. Well, then, you may have to work harder to assert your right to speak up. But there is much to be gained by choosing to overcome your default personality traits, shifting gears, and striving to develop a more effective way of communicating.

Aaron Spencer of Pizzeria Uno adds, "Candor, transparent communications, and timeliness are critical attributes as a professional and ones that must be embraced by nice guys looking to

achieve success. Deferral of these key elements will often introduce complications in the future if not handled appropriately."
Taking these steps will allow overly nice guys to develop the necessary speak-up skills.

Begin by practicing in areas where the intimidation factor is
lower and then build up to situations that are more complex. Ultimately, you'll reach a point where you naturally suppress your
feeling of intimidation and just speak up. Fear is relevant only if
you give it power and, in this case, the power isn't real—it's in
your imagination.

Some people find effective ways to "trick" themselves into being extroverted. Leigh, a magazine publisher, imagines that she's
putting on her "armor" to go to battle. She says the armor trans-
forms her from a shy, introverted person into a courageous, out-
spoken professional.

Roy, the president of a media company who is shy by nature,
gets himself psyched before an important event by imagining—
like an actor—that he's playing the role of a successful, confident
executive. By assuming the qualities of your desired "persona,"
you can take your "self" out of the scene, engage, and "become"
the person who will best serve the interests of your company and
your career.

Late in his career, the great Sir Laurence Olivier still got stage
fright before performances. But he didn't let it keep him from
performing at the highest level. If you've done your homework
(prepare) and discern what's appropriate in a given moment (calibrate), then you'll likely connect with your audience when you
make the choice to speak up (engage).

In the following story, Meryl's new coworker created an extremely volatile and difficult dynamic. Initially, she spoke up on
behalf of her opinions and ideas. Eventually, she would need to
speak up on behalf of her own performance and job security.

### Playing Time

Meryl enjoyed her job leading the English as a Second Language program within her Ohio school system. She was excited when they hired Ann as a new district coordinator. Ann would be her peer, and she looked forward to collaborating with her to create new ideas to help the program grow. Shortly after Ann was hired, however, Meryl became concerned. Whenever she spoke up, made suggestions, or asked questions of Ann, she was met with defensiveness or ignored altogether. This was confusing. In the spirit of collaboration, she set up a meeting with Ann and, in as nonthreatening a way as possible, tried to discuss various issues that were on the table. It didn't go well. Meryl's open, honest, direct approach seemed to make Ann feel even more threatened and insecure, which led to uncomfortable and unproductive dialogue.

Afterward, Meryl decided to take a step back and take stock of the situation to see if she could better calibrate her approach. Striving to be nice and defuse the situation with Ann, she tried various approaches, including asking her to a friendly lunch, bringing her a rose as a gesture of "peace," and trying to convey the message "Relax! I'm not a threat."

Unfortunately, the situation went from bad to worse as she learned from colleagues that Ann was making slanderous comments and accusations about her to numerous people behind her back, including the superintendent. Meryl was shocked and hurt—certain that she hadn't done anything to deserve this unfair treatment. It wasn't in her nature to be a fighter or self-promoter—she was uncomfortable speaking up in that way. She didn't want to "fight fire with fire." But she realized that the situation was engaging her on a whole different level.

Meryl could see that she would need to shift gears and speak up in many different ways in order to preserve her reputation and her job. She was confident, however, that she could do it in ways that would be productive, effective, and in alignment with her own values. She started by making it a habit to record everything that transpired between her and Ann. She gathered copies of her records and performance reviews from the various schools for which she worked. She enlisted the help of trusted colleagues by asking for letters of reference from those who knew and respected her. And, finally, she enlisted the help of a neutral third party to mediate and kept the superintendent informed about the process and how it would unfold. When the day arrived for the mediation, Meryl was so prepared and had so much rational, objective data to support her positions that Ann's subjective sniping was made to look petty and shallow by comparison. As they engaged in dialogue, Ann's position folded like a house of cards, as her irrational position was untenable. She realized that it was in her best interest to work with Meryl or she might put her own position at risk. With the mediator, they found common ground and laid out a framework for future collaboration.

Even with a reasonable amount of wisdom, calibration, and engagement, speaking up may not go well. Occasionally there are times, like Meryl's situation with Ann, where you have to go above and beyond the call of duty to engage in a serious way to stick up for yourself and look out for your best interests—without going overboard and engaging in overly emotional interpersonal warfare. Even football players—who are encouraged to be aggressive—often talk about "staying within themselves" so that they can be clear, focused, and reasoned while in the midst of athletic competition. They're jacked up, but they're calm, too—the calm in the midst of the storm.

## NICE GUY WHIPLASH: Speaking Up

When it comes to speaking up, the ramifications of Nice Guy Whiplash can be quick, dramatic, and messy. Often, the *desire* to speak up precedes the knowledge of *how* to speak up effectively.

Speaking up in inappropriate, inaccurate, or misguided ways creates even bigger problems and challenges. Just as you don't deserve to be intimidated, neither should you intimidate anyone else. This can be a hard balance to achieve while you are developing your speaking-up sea legs.

From words come actions. From actions come ramifications. When it comes to speaking up, Nice Guy Whiplash can play out in numerous ways, including the following:

1. *Raw Comments.* Sometimes the overly nice guy—having felt unheard or pushed around for months or years—impulsively decides that *now* is the time to speak, and without thinking he/she blurts out a barely cooked opinion at the most inappropriate moment. We might amend our earlier statement "Let your opinions be heard" by saying "Let your intelligent, well-thought-out opinions be heard." All thoughts need not be shared with others the moment they come to mind. Instead, *prepare* yourself by developing your opinions in a thoughtful way. Not all of them deserve to see the light of day in front of an audience—only your better ones do.

2. *Time Warps.* An uncooked comment might not be so bad if it happened during a casual moment between friends. The overly nice guy who is unaccustomed to speaking up, however, often has really bad timing. An important presentation to the VP or CEO is not the best time to try out your new skill. First, be sure that you have *prepared* and done the research. Then engage with a peer to ensure that you're comfortable speaking about the topic. And,

most of all, *calibrate* yourself to the situation, always being mindful of what is appropriate and effective in the moment.

3. *Speak-Up Diarrhea.* Once they get a taste of speaking up, some overly nice guys can't shut up. Speaking up becomes an ego trip from which they never return. They dominate conversations and meetings and lose the ability to be inclusive of the opinions of others. Lacking awareness of the situation and audience, they are not *well calibrated* to their environment. It can lead to bad feelings or even to being tuned out by colleagues.

4. *Overstating Your Case.* As they say, "Pick your battles" and "Don't make mountains out of molehills." Overly nice guys who are new to expressing their opinions sometimes struggle with discerning when to draw the line and when to let it go. Learning to be savvy and discern how hard to push is an essential part of speaking up effectively. And when you have only "six silver bullets," it's important to learn that every single opinion need not be fought tooth and nail. For instance, after expressing a new idea or point of view, it may be best to let it sit with an audience and let them digest it. You can then revisit it at a later date and tactfully push for your idea again with renewed energy and perhaps a different approach. Finding a healthy balance is the key.

## NICE COMPANY STRATEGIES
# Speaking Up and Speaking Out

Many overly nice guys elect to remain quiet when confronted with a difficult situation. Like the townspeople in *The Emperor's New Clothes* who kept quiet because they were afraid to tell the emperor he was naked, overly nice guys in the business world are often afraid to speak up and tell the truth because they're fearful of reprisals or hurting people's feelings. This inability or unwillingness to speak up has a significant negative impact on business. Bright ideas, opinions, and input are repressed, and time is wasted. It becomes a conspiracy of silence.

In an NGS (Nice Guy Strategies) survey, business owners estimated that overly nice behavior like this adversely impacts the bottom line by 6 to 10 percent. George Gendron, *Inc.* magazine's former editor in chief, agrees with this assessment. "And over the long term," he adds, "I can see that—for most organizations—the negative impact is much more profound than that."

The bottom line: It is incumbent upon leaders to help overly nice guys learn how to speak up effectively. Companies need to build and nurture a corporate culture that encourages speaking up. This can be accomplished by utilizing strategies that systematically teach speak-up skills. For overly nice guys in your organization, it is simply not enough to spout obvious platitudes like "Get tougher" or "Just do it." They ultimately miss the mark because they are much too general and lack the detailed strategies and support that overly nice guys desperately need.

The following corporate strategies can be employed to help encourage speaking up.

### NICE COMPANY STRATEGY: Creating a Speak-Up Environment

Companies must actively promote a "Speak-Up Environment," where speaking up is rewarded and employees are not afraid of being reprimanded, scorned, or embarrassed. The establishment of such a corporate culture allows for solutions to be reached more creatively and effectively. The focal point of discussions becomes solving the problem instead of being unnecessarily concerned with misspeaking. Many companies struggle with this concept.

*The Art of Innovation*, written by Tom Kelley with Jonathan

Littman, provides an in-depth look at the success of IDEO, Tom Kelley's industrial design company. IDEO has frequently been recognized as one of the leading organizations in innovation. Central to their methodology is the importance of employees speaking up and sharing their thoughts. In their initial brainstorming sessions, all ideas are recorded and given due consideration. Ideas are more likely to come forward if people aren't concerned with their ideas being harshly judged or shot down. On subsequent passes, ideas are then objectively evaluated so that the cream can rise to the top. By quickly deliberating and cultivating large quantities of ideas and then identifying which ones have merit, they can progress efficiently, effectively, and creatively. Whether at the beginning of the process or further down the road, speaking up and focusing on results are central themes that help them achieve success.

Bill Allen of Outback Steakhouse learned an important lesson early in his career. He began speaking up to avoid the "death by committee" experience he endured at one of his earlier positions in a very large company. "Death by committee" meant participants felt stifled because of concerns about saying the "right" things at meetings, which in many cases were executive-laden gatherings. Attendees were inhibited about introducing new ideas—be they good or bad—because they sensed that ideas that were not introduced by a senior executive would likely not be well received. This unspoken mandate suppressed creativity. Meetings consistently proved to be ineffective vehicles for meaningful dialogue because everyone was afraid to speak up.

This experience served as a catalyst for change for Allen, who learned the importance of promoting a Speak-Up Environment and giving employees a voice. Allen believes that "supporting the ability to speak up will allow employees to feel genuinely comfortable in expressing new ideas without the fear of reprisal." He incorporated this mentality into the culture of his subsequent businesses. He made it clear that he expected to hear from all team members regardless of rank—even when the news was not good (or *especially* when the news was not good). This allowed employees to feel genuinely comfortable about expressing new ideas without the fear of reprisal.

Here are a few techniques that can be used to cultivate a Speak-Up Environment within your organization:

**BILL ALLEN, CEO,
OUTBACK STEAKHOUSE**

Supporting the ability to speak up will allow employees to feel genuinely comfortable in expressing new ideas without the fear of reprisal.

1. *Speak Up through Questions.* Organizations typically promote the notion of speaking up when people have new ideas. This can present a problem if people don't necessarily feel that they have a brilliant idea at the moment. An effective way to get people engaged in brainstorming and dialogue is to encourage them to ask questions. As Jim Turley of Ernst & Young says, "When you're asking questions, you're going to look smarter." The questions may come verbally or in writing during meetings or other activities. Acknowledge these questions and be sure to recognize the people who posed them. Dr. Tori Haring-Smith of Washington & Jefferson College likes to ask directed questions. "It fosters ownership," she says. "For instance, I might say, 'I hear that you want us to raise tuition radically this year. Let us explore that for a minute. Which of our currently enrolled students would not be able to attend if we did that? Do we care? What will this do to our reputation?' So I go through a series of questions trying to point people in the right direction rather than quickly saying, 'No. Don't you realize the ramifications if we did that?'

"Instead of telling them what to do," Haring-Smith adds, "directed questions allow people to see my point of view and feel ownership of the outcome. *They feel as if it's theirs rather than mine.* So I tend to occupy myself with finding the right question to ask them rather than trying to frame a persuasive argument."

2. *Dinner-Table Conversations.* If the atmosphere within your organization is one of rigid or semirigid formality, strive to loosen it up. Many people—especially overly nice guys—are more comfortable expressing themselves in relaxed settings where people can share different perspectives on a more informal basis. Herb Kelleher finds this to be an important technique at Southwest Airlines. "Creating an atmosphere in which people feel comfortable speaking their minds without running the risk of offending people is enormously important. In order to accomplish this, make them feel like part of the family. You want people to feel free to have a dinner-table conversation; some people are like the quiet, reclusive kid who doesn't say much in the classroom but babbles at dinner."

Every organization will have a unique culture and blend of environments that either cultivate or suppress a Speak-Up Environment. Regardless, making a conscious effort to create a positive environment where everyone—including overly nice guys—can share opinions and ideas can have a dramatic impact on stimulating creativity, productivity, profitability, and employee satisfaction.

### NICE COMPANY STRATEGY: On the Corporate Stage

Corporate speak-up strategies should scale up or down to adapt to various "corporate stages" that exist in a business. A corporate stage can be as small as a two-person meeting or as large as a public presentation that reaches out to hundreds or thousands of people. It is incumbent upon your organization to encourage employees—especially overly nice guys—to gain experience on those stages in order to develop a level of comfort and competence around speaking up.

Speaking on a *small stage*—one-on-one or in small meetings—is typically an interactive experience with bidirectional communication. In some cases, these meetings are planned—with agendas and identified outcomes. In other cases, they may be hallway chats or water-cooler conversations that are less formal. In either case, overly nice guys will need to develop the appropriate skills to speak up appropriately and meaningfully to add value. To prepare for a small-stage interaction, organizations can help overly nice guys by defining meaningful techniques for these meetings, including the following:

1. *Curveballs.* Overly nice guys have a tendency to get stuck or caught up when presented with an issue that they have not considered. Teach them how to plan for deviation and opposition (i.e., "curveballs") when they speak to smaller groups, including the ability to be nimble and offer alternatives or variations on the key ideas presented.

2. *Avoid Tangentitis.* One of the positive aspects of the small stage is that overly nice guys feel more comfortable sharing their thoughts more openly and liberally. A downside to this informality is that discussions can lose focus and follow too many tangents. Overly nice guys are notorious in this regard; they often don't want to "derail" a good thought process. Train them to focus on the desired outcome of the conversation and manage meetings as effectively as possible. Brian Scudamore of 1-800-GOT-JUNK? knows the importance of keeping his staff—especially the overly nice guys—focused and productive in

meetings. He encourages his employees to ask themselves questions such as these: Did I get out of this meeting exactly what I wanted? Were clear communication and explicit expectations set and followed?

Speaking up on the *big stage*—to medium- or large-sized groups—likely introduces a one-way communication experience for both the speaker and the audience. This entails a more structured and less free-flowing exchange. Whether the overly nice guy is the lead speaker or one of several, he or she will need help developing the confidence and poise necessary to excel in these situations—especially since they often have a strong fear of failing or being perceived as unknowledgeable. Companies can help their employees in numerous ways when speaking up on the big stage, including public-speaking classes, coaching, and joint-presentation techniques. Here are several techniques that can also help:

1. *Breathe and Speak.* At times, before addressing a large crowd, the mind is willing but the body is not. As the speaker tenses up, hands get clammy, the stomach ties up in knots, and, believe it or not, breathing almost comes to a standstill. Before addressing a large audience on an important topic, it is a *really* good idea to have plenty of air in your lungs and a body that is in good, working order. Offstage, warm up and do various exercises to stay loose, including deep-breathing techniques to keep your lungs (and body) full and strong.

2. *Irrelevant Speaking.* When people are seriously challenged to speak up, it can help to practice speaking on topics that are completely irrelevant to your business. Invite them to speaking clubs or casual presentations—similar to Toastmasters International—where they can present on a topic that is of importance to them. They'll be looser, have more fun, and increase their confidence when they practice in low-pressure situations. Over time, this will

help them develop the fortitude and confidence to speak up on matters of relevance.

3. *The Bad Comes with the Good.* Even when speaking up in large groups, overly nice guys will find it easier to deliver good news. Unfortunately, sometimes bad news has to be shared. This is a huge challenge for overly nice guys, who really want to be popular—or at least unobtrusive. So their default behavior is to either delay sharing bad news or bail out and pass the buck to someone else. Because of this, emphasis should be placed on developing the ability to deliver messages that are not popular.

In one particular case, a software company had a CFO named Jim who was a self-admitted overly nice guy. When the company was doing well, he felt comfortable addressing large groups. However, when the company went through a challenging period, he was unable to muster the necessary skills to share the disappointing results with the employees. Ultimately, he realized that his avoidance was causing him to be ineffective in his job. He asked his CEO for some coaching around this issue. The coaching consisted of several one-on-one meetings in which they reviewed the material and decided the most effective way to deliver the information. They agreed on the importance of the presentation being authentic, accurate, and forward thinking to demonstrate how the company would do better. Eventually, they jointly delivered the tough news in an appropriate and effective way. Jim summoned the necessary honesty and courage to deliver the information with integrity and confidence.

Utilizing these techniques on a regular basis will help overly nice guys develop a comfort level for speaking up in different circumstances. The notion of a "corporate stage" provides overly nice guys with a frame of reference and a way of scaling and calibrating their approach to a variety of situations and environments.

## Chapter Summary

### NICE GUY MOTIVES AND SYMPTOMS

**Fear of Being Judged**
Overly nice guys frequently are much too concerned about the opinions and criticism of others and the judgments (real or perceived) that often result.

**Sense of Unworthiness**
Low self-confidence is common among overly nice guys. They are often unsure about the validity of their opinions and, at times, don't feel worthy of expressing them.

**Lack of Confidence in Speaking Abilities**
It can be a challenge for overly nice guys to speak up appropriately, accurately, and effectively. This lack of confidence in what to say and how to say it often leads them to remain silent rather than risk saying the wrong thing.

**Inability to Really Listen**
Learning how to be a good listener can be challenging. Sometimes overly nice guys hear only what they want to hear as opposed to what is really being said—especially if it's bad news.

### NICE GUY STRATEGIES

**Prepare**
You should take the necessary steps to prepare for speaking up in front, within, or outside your organization. Don't feel you can speak up only on an ad hoc basis.

**Calibrate**
Learn about your audience and align your style of speaking with what works best with them.

**Engage**  Once prepared and calibrated, you must now move forward and speak up as appropriate.

### NICE COMPANY STRATEGIES

**Cultivate a Speak-Up Environment**  Proactively develop and maintain an environment within your organization that provides a comfortable setting for overly nice guys to speak up.

**On the Corporate Stage**  Help overly nice guys in your company develop the necessary skills to speak up in a planned and ad hoc capacity and to do so for small, medium, and large groups.

## CHAPTER 3

YOU HAVE THE RIGHT TO:

# Set Boundaries

SET THEM
AND
RESPECT THEM

> "Good fences make good neighbors."
>
> —*Robert Frost*

## NICE GUY SYNDROME
# The Challenge of Setting Boundaries

Many nice people believe that "it is better to give than to receive." But when does giving become a liability in the business world? And how can a nice guy withstand a barrage of unwanted input, inappropriate criticism, or incessant requests from others?

Because overly nice guys tend to be people pleasers, they often find it hard to push back when an unreasonable request is made. The idea of saying no seems almost impossible. Without boundaries, they are slaves to the whims of others. But when the time is taken to set a boundary, we create a decision point that allows us to evaluate if someone's request—for attention, for time, for effort, for money, etc.—warrants a *yes, no,* or *maybe.* We can weigh the merit of the request against our own needs, priorities, and desires. Within the workplace, we add to the equation consideration for the needs and priorities of our team and our organization.

Overly nice guys struggle with boundaries. They don't value

their time and talent appropriately and tend to give them away without proper consideration. Frequently, they don't take the time to weigh a decision—and if they do, they inappropriately give more credence to the needs of others than they give to their own. They continually wish to please others regardless of the impact that doing so may have upon them. At other times, they know that they'd rather not acquiesce to the request—but do so anyway—and resent doing so afterward. Their inability to stick up for themselves and look after their own self-interests and well-being is the culprit.

To find the right balance, overly nice guys must set boundaries for themselves and others. Otherwise, the giving never stops.

## The Stories

The following two stories are based on real events and illustrate a few of the challenges with boundaries that nice guys face in the business world. What would *you* do? Would you set boundaries in these situations? How might you go about establishing them? Would you be able to commit to them over time? Would others respect them? It's not always easy to discern what is "right" or "wrong," and the ramifications of setting clear boundaries (or not setting them) can be significant—not only for the nice guy but also for those who are influenced and affected by the nice guy's behavior and choices.

### The Disservice of Service

Shelby, a young professor at a large, prestigious public university on the East Coast, was a good colleague and hard worker. She was hired because of her strong scholastic record in a PhD program at a prestigious university and her budding research and publication program. From the beginning, she tried her best to be a good citizen and do more than her share of committee work. As is the norm at prominent research universities, her responsibilities involved teaching, research, and service. She knew when she took the job that the old "publish or perish" norm was alive and well, and tried to continue building on the publication record she had successfully begun in her graduate program.

At the same time—because of her conscientiousness and strong work ethic—Carlos, the department chair, and several other more senior professors and administrators often came to her, requesting that she serve on a variety of committees at the university, college, and department levels. Over time, she found herself heavily involved in curriculum committees, new faculty search committees, various gender and diversity committees, and other student advisory and guidance committees. Clearly her heavy level of committee work was well above the norm for a new assistant professor.

Shelby had managed to do a good job in the classroom—receiving consistently strong teaching evaluations from her students—and was recognized as a top service contributor. However, she had not been able to find adequate time for her research. Her publication record suffered. While she really enjoyed research and was genuinely good at it, Shelby had not applied the needed time to excel in this area because she had dedicated too much effort to serving the requests of others. Consequently, when she underwent the college's standard pretenure review several years before she faced her actual tenure decision, she had published only two articles. Although she had several projects in progress, her record was well below department and college expectations.

Nevertheless, hoping that her service and teaching would carry the day, she was surprised when Carlos regretfully delivered the bad news. The department senior faculty had met and decided that if her research performance did not significantly improve, they simply could not support her tenure case. They had decided, with approval from the dean's office, to put her on probation with the expectation that she would significantly improve her performance in the area of research—or face denial of tenure and dismissal. Because she had not set boundaries with others in the area of committee service, she had fallen victim to her own attempts at being a good citizen (and "overniceness"), and her job was now in jeopardy.

### Frank and Ted's Not-So-Excellent Adventure

Frank had been a training manager and lead trainer within his company for more than eight years. He considered himself to be relatively savvy about designing and implementing various training programs created and offered by his department. In addition, he was widely considered to be an expert in delivering his own training materials on a variety of topics, including teamwork, communication, and managing conflict. About a year earlier, Ted, the new HR manager, had been brought into the organization. Ted had a charismatic personality, an engaging personal demeanor, and a strong résumé, and Frank had every expectation that they would work well together. The first few months went smoothly. Ted seemed to recognize Frank's significant experience and allowed him the discretion to do his job in the effective way that he always had.

However, within the last few weeks, Ted had become increasingly involved in the details of the work of the training department—despite having a very limited background in training. He had also begun to express his opinions more actively about how Frank should be organizing and delivering his training sessions. In fact, Frank began to see Ted's behaviors as a form of intrusive micromanagement.

At the same time, Ted was an advocate of open communication with his staff, even if it meant challenging his ideas. He often checked in with Frank for his views on how things were going and requested feedback and suggestions about possible changes in the HR function related to corporate training. Nevertheless, Frank resisted openly discussing his concerns with Ted about his increasing boundary-violating behavior. As a result, things continued to get worse. Over time, Ted frequently sat in on Frank's and other trainers' sessions unannounced and delivered increasingly pointed feedback regarding changes he thought should be made. In general, Ted had placed under siege what Frank considered his professional domain within the company.

The final straw in Frank's mind occurred one afternoon when he was leaning back in a chair in his office pondering some key design issues for an upcoming corporate-wide training program. Lost in his thoughts—just as he was beginning to envision a creative solution to a transitional piece at the center of the program—he heard Ted's half-joking voice from the hallway saying, "Don't we give you enough to do around here?" Frank instinctively reached for a file on his desk and opened it to create an immediate appearance of activity. But the interruption and the implication—even if in jest—that his engaging in creative thought was viewed as a form of loafing was disturbing to Frank.

Nevertheless, continuing his pattern, Frank did not mention it later when Ted once again checked in with him inviting feedback and suggestions for change. He was not able to go beyond his tendency to act nice, even when feeling quite put off by the boundary violation he was feeling with Ted's management style. And Frank's morale and motivation (and the effectiveness of his training sessions) began to suffer.

## The Motives and Symptoms

Both of these situations contain seemingly good reasons to avoid enforcing boundaries in the spirit of "being nice." In Shelby's case, she wanted to be a good colleague and provide worthwhile service for her department and for the university. Consequently, she ended up serving everyone except herself. And Frank apparently was more concerned that his communications with Ted not lead to overt conflict that he would find uncomfortable. As a result, he was able to continue to work and interact with his new boss without any apparent relationship breakdown, at least in the short run. But he has, unintentionally, contributed to an ever-worsening situation that will likely lead to a more complete relationship failure down the road.

Clearly these kinds of well-intentioned motives can lead nice people to choose ineffectual behavior and unhealthy relationships with very real consequences for them and their organizations. In Shelby's case, not only is her department missing out on the research contributions she is capable of making, but she may soon lose her job and her colleagues could lose her services altogether. On top of that, her department would be faced with the onerous task of recruiting, hiring, and orienting a brand-new person. And Frank is increasingly being filled with the kind of resentment and negative feelings that could lead to more destructive conflict with Ted in the future. This lack of boundary-protecting behavior, which ultimately can lead to reduced effectiveness and long-term success, is a central part of the Nice Guy Syndrome.

What are the nice guy symptoms related to neglecting boundaries? There are many, involving various related behaviors and emotions, but we highlight three in particular:

1. *People Pleasing.* Overly nice people have a tendency to try to please everyone—except themselves. They often say yes to requests

from others and expect that their niceness will be appreciated and not go unrewarded. They seem to think that acting in a pleasing way— often with polite silence—and allowing others to invade their boundaries is more important than getting the issues out on the table. This can lead to a variety of negative consequences, such as bad morale and weak performance.

2. *Victim Mentality.* When their boundaries are under siege as a result of trying to please others, overly nice guys often perceive themselves as being victimized by the situation. This only further interferes with their ability to be effective. There are times, of course, when people have reason to be upset and to feel that they are being unfairly treated. Yet, focusing on (and feeling upset about) being a victim will only make things worse and often leads to unhealthy feelings associated with being a victim—such as powerlessness, self-pity, and bitterness.

3. *Taking Things Personally.* A big deterrent to overly nice guys setting boundaries is that they have a tendency to take challenge and disagreement personally. An overly nice guy with weak boundaries is easily stung by the unsolicited advice and biting criticism of others. Instead of objectively considering people's opinions and pushing back when appropriate, they lose the ability to evaluate the situation. They are quick to assume that if someone else said it, it must be true. And, most damaging of all—due to an inability to separate their work from their self-image—they frequently assume that all criticism is personal and allow it to damage their self-esteem.

To sum up, one of the most challenging skills to learn in life is how to find a healthy balance between being responsive to the requests of others and protecting ourselves through setting and maintaining appropriate boundaries. Ironically, Shelby's lack of boundary management—in the spirit of being both good and nice in the area of committee service—unintentionally resulted in her letting her colleagues down by not adequately contributing to research. And Frank's attempts to be "nice" in his relationship with his boss have actually put him on the road to a much more significant relationship breakdown. Frank's boss has overstepped appropriate boundaries and is becoming a crippling distraction and demotivator, rendering Frank ineffective in doing his work. Frank has tried to remain civil and "nice," but clearly some action is needed to set and maintain healthy boundaries before things get worse.

Poorly defined boundaries are not unusual for overly nice guys. It can be difficult for them to recognize how choosing in the present moment to be a bit less nice and more assertive can positively affect things later—and in ways that ultimately turn out to be more authentically nice. The good news is that there are several nice guy strategies that can help.

NICE GUY STRATEGIES

# The Importance of a Good Boundary

Boundary setting is one of the most important and challenging skills for nice guys to develop. We can't avoid interacting with people and making decisions—large and small—about the things that are asked of us minute by minute, hour by hour: "Will you do this project for me?" "Can you finish it by five o'clock?" "Will you please fix the copier?" "Can you work late and finish that report?" "Would you be willing to go to Dallas tomorrow and make that presentation for me?" "We're giving your group added responsibilities, but you can't increase head count. No problem, right?"

How we respond to these ongoing series of requests at work

defines our style and aptitude for setting boundaries. At times it may be subtle, such as asking for more time to complete a project instead of frantically striving to finish it under the constraints of an unreasonable deadline. At other times, it might be more significant, such as assertively confronting someone, rigorously protecting your time, or firmly defining your job description, target market, or annual deliverables.

Nice guys—and those with whom they interact—benefit when healthy boundaries are set. We offer insights about how to set boundaries in a healthy and productive way, ensuring that our own interests (and those of others and the organization) are being equally and reasonably served. Boundaries vary in nature, so overly nice guys must astutely identify those that suit a particular person and situation. And when overly nice guys find that their niceness is being abused, they must define, defend, and reinforce their boundaries in order to protect their productivity and foster effective relationships.

Here are several strategies that will help unravel this mystery and aid in the creation of boundaries.

## NICE GUY STRATEGY: Sorting

When your boundaries are under siege, it's easy to feel a lack of control. In the mind of an overly nice guy, the choices are few because he or she is at the whim (or mercy) of others. They take it personally and feel victimized by the way they are being treated. "How could he do this to me?" they grumble. "That's not my job. I don't have time for this!" But defenseless and lost, the overly nice guy keeps plugging away, like Atlas trudging up the hill with the weight of the world (or the weight of responsibility for the project or deadline) on his shoulders. Invariably, the overly nice guy says yes and assumes responsibility for a task or problem.

Why? Because someone asked (or demanded) that he does so—and he's just a guy who can't say no.

How can you gain some semblance of control in challenging situations when your boundaries are under attack?

The first step is to shift your perspective by depersonalizing the problem. Depersonalization entails untangling the objective situational challenges from the subjective personalities (and feelings) involved. It isn't always easy, especially if one has a long, frustrating history with a boss or colleague. But a rational view of the problem frees you from the debilitating emotional quagmire and allows you to regain control of the situation and yourself.

### Monster on the Rampage

Ella worked as a marketing manager for a large software company. She reported to Rod, the VP of marketing. He was a very charismatic person with big energy, a big personality, and a big temper. He was also a narcissistic person who essentially wasn't hard-wired to consider the needs and feelings of others. He was, however, *very* attuned to his own needs and demanded that they be met at all times—or else.

Ella described her experience: "Working for Rod was like riding a roller coaster. The highs were really exciting and fun, but the lows were brutal. I never knew what to expect from day to day. It was almost impossible for anyone in our group to have good boundaries because Rod would toss them aside as if they were made of paper, like Godzilla in the old Japanese movies. In fact, his nickname around the office was 'Rodzilla.'

"It got really bad one spring after our company announced poor quarterly earnings. Rodzilla was on the rampage. Among other things, he started leaving angry, irrational messages once a week on my voice mail, seemingly blaming me and/or my group for everything. It got to the point where I felt so beaten up that all rational thought got thrown out the window. I began to believe that everything he said *must* be true because he was my boss . . . and because he said everything so loudly and so forcefully.

"I started to see a business coach, and during our sessions I played the phone messages from Rod that I'd saved. My coach helped me learn to not take these messages personally and see that what he was saying was *not* all about me, or my group. In fact, *most* of what Rod said was about *him*. He was projecting a lot of his own personal baggage onto us for a variety of reasons, perhaps due to the amount of pressure that he was under along with the challenges that I know he was facing in his personal life. We were easy targets. Since we put up little or no resistance, it became a pattern. Ultimately, I could choose to stay or choose to go, but the most important thing for me to learn was to depersonalize the situation and be more objective about my feelings and responses."

Ella gained valuable wisdom from her business coach. *Don't* take everything personally. *It's not all about you.* Choosing to stay on your side of the street and focus on what is your responsibility can be extremely liberating and empowering. This is especially true for overly nice guys, who often feel victimized by circumstances and instinctively want to please others. Do not assume that the words or actions of others are motivated by some secret desire to impose upon you or "get" you. While the jerks or SOBs of the world can occasionally be malicious, they are much more likely to be insensitive, unthinking, or just plain clueless in the ways they deal with other people. Try to objectively treat the action as simply that—an action—and refrain from assigning a sinister ulterior motive to the behavior.

Once Ella grasped that Rod's words were not 100 percent gospel truth and that she shouldn't just take them at face value, it became easier for her to not take his diatribes personally. On the other hand, Ella's coach cautioned that Rod's input would sometimes have some nuggets of value, based upon his intelligence and years of marketing experience. Perhaps Ella and her group had room for improvement and could have an even greater impact on the company's success and quarterly earnings.

How can Ella have healthy boundaries, be more self-aware, and learn where she has room for personal growth? We advocate a process that we call *sorting*.

Sorting is a rigorously honest assessment of a situation. It helps discern what is "mine" and what is "yours." Think of it as putting each situation through an objective filter and then using percentages to assign ownership and responsibility. You must be brutally honest with yourself or this process will have little or no value. It can be helpful to do it with an impartial third person—someone who is aware and astute but also willing to ask you tough questions about your culpability in a situation.

As an example, let's do some sorting on a phone message that Rod left on Ella's voice mail. The message exclaimed, "Being a month late on that product launch last quarter was a disaster! If that happens again, there'll be hell to pay!" Sorting through the message and its explicit and implicit meanings, Ella could honestly say that she had very little control over the schedule of the product launch. Until Engineering officially released the product, she couldn't finalize the press tour or finish the marketing communications. And Rod was less than timely with his approvals on the various programs that were proposed for the launch—mostly due to the fact that he was preoccupied with opening the new Asian office and buying a new boat.

However, Ella had to admit that she didn't proactively speak up, wave the flag, and alert the launch team as to how these delays would affect the schedule. Many things were left unspoken and many assumptions were made. Ella didn't want to be the "bad guy" and give the bad news that no one wanted to hear. So she said nothing—which eventually led to large amounts of chaos and frustration for many people. She had to admit that while approximately 70 percent of the responsibility was not hers, 30 percent was. There was plenty that she could learn from the experience—lessons that would help her become a better manager and stronger leader in the future.

### NICE GUY STRATEGY: Fortify

Once nice guys learn to sort difficult requests and situations—and look at them in a more objective and truthful way—the process of fortifying boundaries can begin. How? In a proactive and conscious way, they must *stop* them from crumbling, *know* the value of their time, talent, energy, etc., and *recognize* that there is a significant cost if their boundaries are shoddy and weak.

A crucial first step in creating clear and effective boundaries is the ability to say no. If yes is always the answer to every request, then boundaries don't exist. Control and discretion is lost. Let us be clear: we are not advocating that overly nice guys should *always* say no, or even frequently say no. After all, many requests are reasonable and important and deserve careful consideration. What is vitally important, however, is that overly nice guys are confident that they can say no when necessary—even if it consequently leads to being perceived as unhelpful, selfish, or "wrong."

Because they are eager to be helpful, play the hero, or perhaps just can't say no, overly nice guys become yes-aholics and their boundaries quickly crumble. Joe McGuire, CEO of Tweeter, says "the 'nice guy trap' is caused by somebody who is way too nice, never says no, and takes everything on." This is exacerbated by their tendency to think they need to provide an answer to every request instantly.

One way to effectively combat the tendency to be a yes-aholic and fortify your boundaries is to learn this very important skill: the value of silence. Since silence can often feel uncomfortable or even intolerable, overly nice guys tend to want to fill the gaps with words.

Silence is an extremely valuable tool when used deftly and consciously. It takes many forms. It might be a simple pause— allowing one to collect one's thoughts and offer a meaningful response. At other times, the nice guy might choose to tactically sidestep an issue and refrain from giving an answer, saying something to the effect of, "I'll give some thought to that and get back to you later."

Making the conscious choice *not* to return a phone call immediately can provide nice guys with the extra time and space they need to be more thoughtful with their response or opinion. And in a particularly contentious moment, they might choose to literally call a truce to remove themselves from the situation effectively. They can readdress the issue later, when cooler heads and common sense are more likely to prevail. One successful executive sometimes tells impatient employees who want immediate answers to their requests, "If I have to give you an answer now, the answer is no. If you give me time to consider the request, the answer *might* be yes."

Sometimes nice guys must set boundaries regarding what is appropriate behavior. Enduring abuse from a bullying boss or tyrannical client is never acceptable to a self-respecting nice guy and should never implicitly be considered a part of anyone's job description. To allow a colleague to cross that line is a slippery slope indeed, as Linda experienced in the following story.

### Cruella de Pill

A large book publisher in New York City wanted to expand into smaller specialty markets. To this end, they bought Graybrook, a small publisher in rural Indiana with a long history of success. The parent company sent Alice, an aggressive executive from New York City, to manage this new acquisition. Alice was not pleased with the employees and corporate culture she found at Graybook, nor were her new employees pleased with "Cruella" and her abrasive manner and "whip them until they produce" management style.

In order to bring a higher level of professionalism to Graybrook, Alice hired Linda from out of state to be the creative director and manage the art department.

"Within the first ninety minutes of my first day on the job," recalled Linda, "Alice called me into her office and said, 'I'm not happy with the quality of the employees here. I want you to fire three people by tomorrow. I'm not sure which three. You choose.'"

Linda was floored. "I hadn't even been on the job two hours and she's *telling* me to fire people I don't even know!" she recalled. "Not only was I *completely* lacking the context within which to evaluate anyone, but she was also seriously overstepping boundaries by telling *me* to arbitrarily fire people on my new staff."

In response to Alice's directive, Linda instinctively knew in that moment that she had to make a stand and defend her boundaries. "I have to admit she was intimidating, and mean," she remembered. "I'm a nice person. I really felt like I was out of my element. But somehow I got my wits about me, took a deep breath, and said to her, 'My job is to manage this department, Alice, *not* to be your hatchet man. I need the latitude to do my job as I see fit.'"

It worked. Alice was perturbed that Linda said no, but she grudgingly backed down and, over time, showed her more respect and consideration.

Linda set a firm boundary and asserted the right to do her job and manage her staff. She had to summon the courage to do this in the midst of an intensely challenging situation with a very intimidating boss. By claiming her rights and responsibilities as a manager and saying no to Alice's request to fire employees arbitrarily, Linda fortified her boundaries in significant ways.

### NICE GUY STRATEGY: Prioritize

Once boundaries have been properly fortified, the next step is to learn how to make healthy decisions when requests are made of your time and talent and energy. To do so, overly nice guys must selectively discern when to say yes or no by consciously evaluating and prioritizing everything that's asked.

And don't forget that one of your most important priorities must always be *you.*

At first blush, such a statement seems selfish and egotistical. It's not. If you don't take care of yourself and get your needs met, you're not going to be of much use to anybody, least of all yourself. Consider the advice you receive from a flight attendant during the preflight routine. "In the unlikely event of a sudden loss in cabin pressure, oxygen masks will drop down in front of you. If you are with a small child, first put on your oxygen mask *before* assisting your child."

Why? Obviously, if the parents' needs are not met and they lose consciousness, they will be of no use to their child.

Overly nice guys are often excessively altruistic—always thinking of others and forgetting their own needs. However, if you are consistently miserable, overworked, and unfulfilled in your job (i.e., if you figuratively "lose consciousness"), you are of little use to your employer or yourself. Your effectiveness and success will be stunted or perhaps crippled. Overly nice guys should strive to avoid the tendency to sacrifice their own needs and fulfillment for the sake of unnecessarily pleasing others. Ultimately, being a victim and a martyr does not serve anyone. Work with others to create mutually agreeable goals and deliverables. Take an active role in setting your agenda and defining your priorities.

The following story describes what happens when priorities get muddied and an overly nice guy becomes a martyr.

### The Cover-Up

Tom, thirty-five, managed the marketing group within a medium-sized software company. He loved his job and excelled by most any standard—with the exception of his personal life. He didn't have one. Working nights and weekends was the norm for Tom.

His group's head count stayed flat while the workload increased. "I sacrificed my weekends for months and months," he said, "always believing that things would eventually get better if we could just make it through the latest fire drill . . . the hot product launch, the huge user conference, etc. But it never got better. That's not to say that people didn't appreciate my work and my efforts. They did—and I got lots of strokes. In all honesty, I think I took some sort of perverse pride in being the weekend warrior. Yet, I had also become exhausted and resentful about the fact that I had sacrificed my personal life."

Tom continued, "Then one rainy Saturday, I was at the office and it hit me . . . it *never* would get better. I had, unknowingly, been covering up the problem. By throwing myself at the workload, twenty-four/seven, everything was getting done. Why should they add to head count when everything is getting done 'just fine'? I had to set a boundary and state, 'This is how much work I can do in forty to fifty hours a week.' The only way that the problem—being understaffed—would be exposed was if I *let* some things go undone. Until then, it wouldn't be acknowledged or taken seriously."

Tom then went to his boss, showed her everything that was on his overflowing plate, and discussed what he deemed to be a reasonable workload. "I made *her* prioritize and decide what gets done and what falls off my plate," Tom added. "And voilà! My weekends magically reappeared once again."

Being dedicated and working hard is certainly commendable. Going above and beyond the call of duty by putting in extra hours is necessary at times—and can also be gratifying and fun. However, if it develops into a pattern and becomes the norm, you may have a boundaries problem like Tom. A boundary cannot be honored and respected if it was never set in the first place. Overcommitting your time and energy is not the answer. Achieving a healthy balance in life is.

### NICE GUY WHIPLASH: Setting Boundaries

A completely different boundary problem is when someone goes overboard and becomes extreme in his or her boundary setting. This behavior can take different forms and has a variety of ramifications. Here are some examples:

1. *The Knee-Jerk "No."* Instantly saying no before a request has been considered or priorities have been weighed is not healthy or productive. This knee-jerk response often happens when someone has a history of feeling overworked or taken advantage of.

2. *The Boundary Nazi.* Overreacting to boundary abuse can cause one to become an angry, mean-spirited Boundary Nazi,

personified by rude, inconsiderate behavior and a complete disregard for the needs and feelings of others.

3. *Paranoid Walls.* If one's boundaries have been consistently as-
saulted over time, it can lead to feelings of mistrust, fear, and para-
noia. This paranoid behavior can lead to isolation and the building
of "moats" and "walls" around oneself to keep people (and their
requests) at bay.

## NICE COMPANY STRATEGIES
## A Blueprint for Boundaries

In business, requests for our time and energy continue to grow at
an alarming pace and come from many directions—via meeting
invites, e-mails, voice mails, instant messages, written correspon-
dence, hallway conversations, calendar invites, and others. If not
properly managed, these requests can compromise boundaries
and seriously affect productivity, profitability, and the quality of
work.

Overly nice guys tend to respond to such requests and stimuli
in an ineffective manner. Perhaps they fail to push back on demands for their time or agree to assume responsibility for tasks
that are not theirs. They may be cornered into participating in
lengthy and irrelevant conversations. Or shoddy boundaries may
lead overly nice guys to accept substandard results from subordinates, peers, or their managers. In such situations, they do not
want to "rock the boat" or upset others. They do not take the
time to correct the behavior or kick back the poor-quality deliv-
erable. Instead, they may take it upon themselves to remedy the
situation.

Boundary problems within companies are complicated by the

nature of the employer-employee relationship—in which the overly nice guy feels obligated to comply with all requests—and become even more problematic due to corporate cultures that strongly promote going "the extra mile." The desire to help others can become addictive, like a drug, as they feel compelled to go "above and beyond the call of duty."

Part of the problem stems from the challenge that overly nice guys face shifting from a personal context to a business context. Jon Luther of Dunkin' Brands describes his company as his "Business Family." Luther says, "At Dunkin', we have established 'the Business Family.' The things you would tolerate in your own *personal* family might not be tolerated in our *business* family. It is important that Business Family members remain focused on meaningful *business* results and that clear boundaries are established and protected."

> **JON LUTHER, CEO, DUNKIN' BRANDS**
>
> At Dunkin', we have established "the Business Family." The things you would tolerate in your own *personal* family might not be tolerated in our *business* family.

As previously mentioned, in one of our NGS surveys, business owners indicated that overly nice behavior can adversely impact the bottom line by 6 to 10 percent. George Gendron, *Inc.* magazine's former editor in chief, agrees with the survey results for the short term. However, "over the long term," he says, "I can see that, for most organizations, it's much more profound than that." The bottom line: It is incumbent upon leaders to help overly nice guys establish better boundaries, and here are two strategies that can make a difference.

## NICE COMPANY STRATEGY: Drafting a Blueprint

Overly nice guys need structure (i.e., a blueprint) for establishing boundaries in a meaningful way. For Dunkin' Brands, the Business Family serves as a blueprint for boundaries, one that is designed to optimize success and to impact the bottom line for the company positively.

Teaching overly nice guys how to draft better boundaries can truly make a difference in your organization. In so doing, you will cultivate nice guys who are more productive, effective, and valuable to your company. You can help the overly nice guys in your organization by taking the following steps and drafting a blueprint for better boundaries.

1. *Defining Boundaries That Work.* Boundary definition and strength will vary depending upon the formality, culture, and size of your organization. For a small company, loose boundaries may be necessary since everyone must wear many hats. In these situations, overly nice guys must be cognizant of the role they are playing at any particular time and define boundaries accordingly. For example, assume an engineer in a twenty-person land survey consultancy has been assigned the task of performing quality assurance (QA) work for one week. During that week, a peer asks her to stop the QA effort to help with a separate engineering initiative. As an overly nice guy, she wants to help, yet she must define her boundaries and prioritize. She needs to clear this new task with management so that they can either consciously choose to reprioritize the work or ask her to stick to her original assignment. If her boundaries are sloppy and she tries to wear both hats at the same time, both projects could suffer since it's unlikely that she could give each one the attention and effort it would require.

For a large organization, much more stringent boundaries may be needed in order to support job responsibilities and corporate policies. In these situations, however, there is a danger that companies may become overly enamored with establishing boundaries and ultimately create too many. A very rigid, limiting approach can inhibit creativity and the development of new ideas—neither of which is the goal of well-formulated boundaries.

2. *Protecting Boundaries.* Overly nice guys are often quite productive and effective in their work life until a problem arises and someone asks them to cross a boundary. Their desire to help—or fear of saying no—leads them to quickly compromise their boundaries. When their judgment gets clouded, they may need help deciding which requests are most important. In some cases, their manager might define the priorities. In other cases, the overly nice guy can give it a try and then present the priorities to management for review. The key is to teach overly nice guys first to be aware that a boundary is needed and then to consciously prioritize so that their time, energy, budget, and resources are protected.

Kofax is a global document management software company that employs effective boundary protection in their sales process. Specifically, the software company has defined a policy that states, "No customer references are to be given out until a prospect has committed to moving forward with a purchase." This is an important boundary since the software company doesn't want its existing customers contacted unless the opportunity is legitimate. Despite the definition of this boundary, many of their prospects still prematurely ask Kofax salespeople for reference information. Those salespeople who suffer from Nice Guy Syndrome frequently give in—effectively compromising the process and the boundary. On the other hand, those who adhere to this boundary gain a new level of respect from the company's management team, their peers, and, ultimately, their customers, too. People at first may not like the boundary, but in the long run they'll grow to respect you for it.

3. *Respecting the Boundaries of Others.* Once overly nice guys have defined and protected their boundaries, they need to learn how to avoid impeding on the boundaries of others. In many cases, overly nice guys eagerly offer to help when it's inappropriate and unwelcome—which can become problematic and counterproductive if unchecked. Terry Stinson of Bell Helicopter has noticed that "when the overly nice guy is too aggressive in helping others, it ultimately becomes a nuisance. It can also be perceived as disingenuous." Consequently, it's important to recognize and systemically correct overly nice guys who are oblivious to other people's boundaries.

## NICE COMPANY STRATEGY: Corporate Heroism vs. Corporate Martyrdom

People tend to be impressed when their corporate brethren persevere through difficult circumstances in an effort to serve the interests of the company. Acts of selfless determination and commitment often place these people into an elite group that one might call "Corporate Heroes." In fact, the business battle is often won or lost because of these heroes. Their stories become company legend.

But what happens when Corporate Heroes push themselves too far or in misguided ways? Overly nice guys frequently become "Corporate Martyrs"—people who put forth a similar effort as Corporate Heroes but extend themselves well beyond reasonable boundaries. Rather than working smarter, the Corporate Martyr works harder, going to extremes to help people at the risk of unknowingly hurting themselves and the business. When overly nice guys repeatedly make this mistake, it can be self-destructive and put the company at risk.

When does Corporate Heroism cross the line and become

Corporate Martyrdom? For the overly nice guy, it is too frequent. With the intensity of today's business demands, it is easy for managers to overlook Corporate Martyrdom. Hence, precautions must be taken to denounce it. Boundaries must be put in place to prevent it. Overly nice guys should be monitored and educated on the importance of boundaries and self-preservation. If they are not, they'll likely fall into old habits—leading to a breakdown in priorities, productivity, and effectiveness.

Here are a few examples of Corporate Martyrs.

### Grace, the Project Manager

A project team was assembled for a large consulting project, including a prime contractor and a subcontractor. Working for the subcontractor was Grace and a few developers. The lead for the prime contractor was a technical architect named Kurt. Unfortunately, Kurt was woefully underqualified. Grace noticed this and considered raising a flag to signify that there was a problem. Instead, she decided to be a nice guy and keep it quiet, hoping that Kurt would eventually pull through. As the project entered the home stretch, it was clear that Kurt simply didn't have the horsepower. Grace had to jump in and work numerous hundred-hour weeks. Even so, the written deliverables were delayed. Despite her well-intended efforts, Grace played the martyr. The process and delays also had an adverse impact on all of Grace's other work, which attracted the notice of management. From that point forward, clear boundaries were defined for her and other key resources on all future team-related projects. For added protection, an escalation process was also implemented to flag risky resources.

### Eric, the Technical Architect

Eric was working with his team on a key presentation, which was to be delivered the following day. As the group made their final preparations late at night, Eric offered to go to Kinko's to print out an important diagram for the presentation, which he would bring with him the next morning. At Kinko's, he was told that the printer was broken and that he'd have to drive ten miles to another Kinko's to print his drawing. Instead, he elected to jump in and fix the printer for Kinko's. He was eventually able to fix the machine, but, unfortunately, he had to stay up straight through the night to do it. When Eric arrived the following day, the diagram looked wonderful but Eric was completely exhausted. Had the team leader known that Eric was going to make this ill-advised choice and play the martyr, he would have advised him to stay focused, stick with the task at hand, get the document printed elsewhere, and get a good night's sleep so that he would be rested and sharp the next day.

To avoid disastrous experiences and results such as those of Grace and Eric, it is incumbent upon company management to be on the lookout for Corporate Martyrs. When overly nice guys push themselves beyond reasonable "hero" limits for the company, a guiding hand is needed to ensure that they don't push too far. Managers can draft "Anti-Martyr" boundaries that are well defined and closely monitored. For instance, in a professional services firm, it may be appropriate to define a maximum number of hours that can be billed within a given period. This could have served as a flag in Grace's case. And time sheets can be monitored to ensure that time and energy are being spent in appropriate ways. For a manufacturing organization, a maximum number of patent submissions could be established for every engineer. In the case of a customer service center, call durations may be tracked to determine if the service representatives are being "just a bit" too helpful.

In the end, companies can help their overly nice guys by providing boundaries that prevent them from hurting themselves and their organization. In the process, they should learn to discern the differences between being a martyr and being a hero. When they do so, they effectively get their work done while staying healthy and productive.

## Chapter Summary

### NICE GUY MOTIVES AND SYMPTOMS

**People Pleasing**  Overly nice people have a tendency to try to please everyone except themselves.

**Victim Mentality**  Feeling as though their boundaries are under siege as a result of trying to please others can create the additional burden of victimhood.

**Taking It Personally**  A big deterrent to overly nice guys setting boundaries is that they often have a tendency to take challenges and disagreements personally.

### NICE GUY STRATEGIES

**Sorting**  Depersonalization helps you untangle objective situational challenges from the subjective feelings involved. Sorting is a rigorously honest assessment of a situation that helps discern what is "mine" and what is "yours."

**Fortify**  Do not let boundaries crumble; know the value of your time, talent, energy, and dignity; and recognize that there is a significant cost if your boundaries are shoddy and weak.

**Prioritize**  You must selectively discern when to say yes or no by consciously evaluating and prioritizing everything that's asked of you as well as the work that you are pursuing.

## NICE COMPANY STRATEGIES

**A Blueprint for Boundaries**
From a company perspective, the absence of defined and respected boundaries introduces a high degree of unpredictability that has a destabilizing effect on the business. As a business leader, you must institutionalize the importance of defining and enforcing boundaries for the benefit of the business and all the overly nice guys.

**Heroism vs. Martyrdom**
It is incumbent upon a company's leadership to ensure that the boundaries, which rest between heroism and martyrdom, are well defined and monitored.

## CHAPTER 4

YOU HAVE THE RIGHT TO:

# Confront

ADDRESS ISSUES
DIRECTLY AND
WITHOUT FEAR

> "All of the great leaders have had one characteristic
> in common: it was the willingness to confront unequivocally
> the major anxiety of their people in their time.
> This, and not much else, is the essence of leadership."
> —*John Kenneth Galbraith, U.S. economist*

## NICE GUY SYNDROME
# The Challenge of Confronting

Nice guys need to be able to challenge the people and ideas they encounter at the workplace. This is the basis for the fourth right: *Nice guys have the right to confront.* Nice guys *must* learn to confront issues effectively if they want to achieve a higher level of success in business.

*Confrontation* is *not* a bad word—even though it's often avoided like the plague. Confrontation, in its most positive spirit, involves constructively challenging ideas and getting important issues out on the table in order to deal with them in an open and honest way. In fact, it is an important tool and can become a positive force for innovative business success. Some overly nice guys subconsciously avoid confrontation and hold to the old adage that they learned at a very young age: "Children should be seen and not heard." Overly nice guys may be idealistic, but they aren't children. They needn't be too nice and deferential, reluctant to deliver challenging news, or always afraid of hurting the feelings of others.

Learning how to use confrontation when it is needed is an

important key to greater effectiveness. Overly nice guys can learn to address issues directly with sensitivity, honesty, and empathy while also overcoming their fears. Practical skills and strategies that we share later in this chapter can help nice people effectively challenge others or, when needed, choose to walk away out of strength rather than in retreat.

## The Stories

The following two stories are inspired by actual events and illustrate some of the difficulties nice guys can face in terms of being able to confront others in the business world. These stories provide a look at two distinct contexts but with overlapping circumstances. The first involves a new manager in a large retail firm and the second is from the world of professional sales.

We ask you to consider: What would *you* do? Do you think you would be able to exercise your right to confront in these contexts? How would you act? Why? These are meaningful questions to consider. It's not always easy to know when and how to challenge others or exactly what is happening and what is called for in difficult situations at work. And the ramifications of choosing to confront (or not to confront) can be significant for the nice guy and others affected by the situation.

### No Parking

Aaron was in the franchise restaurant business in New England. A man with a start-up business named Braylon approached him at a conference. He was interested in Aaron's thoughts on his new restaurant business. "I have always believed that what goes around comes around," Aaron said. "However, in one case what came back around was a kick in the teeth." Aaron scheduled a lunch with Braylon and ended up spending considerable time with him over the next few months—introducing him to landlords, builders, operating people, etc. "We also developed a personal relationship," remembered Aaron, "and had dinner together a number of times. I even had him and his family to our home. I continued to help him for several years and even introduced him to people for additional financing.

"At one point he asked if I would mind one of his restaurants being in the same area with one of mine. I explained that it was a big trade area and he should be there—but I would *not* like him in the same parking lot sharing our customer traffic." A year later, Aaron found out—through word on the street—that not only had Braylon done a deal in the one center that they had specifically discussed, but he was also pursuing locations in multiple centers where Aaron was a tenant. "I found the disrespect for my assistance astonishing. Being a nice guy certainly didn't help in this situation."

### Older . . . but Not Wiser

Casey represented his company's products and services to a variety of corporate clients. Despite being one of the younger members of the sales team, at age twenty-eight Casey already had a solid five years of experience under his belt. Typically, client calls were made in teams of two. Casey had always appreciated the synergy that frequently resulted from this team approach. And when he was paired with Hank, a newly hired older salesman in his midforties who had been in sales for nearly twenty years, Casey expected a similar experience.

At first, Casey found Hank to be very personable and motivated. He thought they would make a good team until they made their first official sales call on a key client of the firm. Since Casey had already worked with the client and had more experience and seniority than Hank within their company, he naturally began the conversation with the client. After some initial pleasant small talk, consistent with normal protocol, he asked the client about his current needs and how they might be able to help. The conversation went on for a few minutes while Casey worked out with the client a mutually agreed-upon plan of product and service offerings for the next quarter. The sales call seemed to be going especially smoothly and successfully.

However, when the client raised a new problem he was having in upgrading a new internal communication system and asked Casey if his firm could help, things soon became difficult. Casey explained to the client that, unfortunately, what was needed was outside their current offerings, but he hoped that they would have a product to offer him in about a year that was under development. As Casey laid out more of the specific details, Hank interrupted him and stated in a confident voice that he would personally find a way to help the client with his problem right away. His tone and manner suggested a superior experience base and aptitude for serving the client that made the younger Casey appear less capable and less influential at the company. After patiently waiting for Hank to finish, Casey then countered as politely as he could. He explained that Hank had just been hired and, while he was already demonstrating a desire to go above and beyond to serve clients, unfortunately, as Casey had stated earlier, their firm currently had nothing to address the client's problem.

When the meeting ended the client was left confused about next steps and Casey and Hank appeared uncoordinated and uninformed about what their firm could and could not offer. When they were alone, Casey puzzled over what had just happened but didn't want to make Hank feel bad, so he just let it go rather than openly challenge him about it. His avoidance of confrontation occurred even though in a recent sales meeting, prior to Hank's hiring, all sales reps were advised to avoid promising clients help in

this area until further notice. Casey expected that his gentle cor-
rection of Hank's comment during the sales call would be enough
to encourage him to mostly just observe client calls for a while
until he gained more experience.

Nevertheless, the situation was repeated several times over the
next few days. Hank would interrupt Casey in a manner that suggested an expertise and importance beyond that of his younger
colleague, even though most of the information he shared was
uninformed and incorrect. As a result Casey was becoming concerned and irritated and believed that he was appearing less competent to his clients. Hank's continuous contradictions of Casey
created an increasingly bad situation for both Casey and his clients. Nevertheless, in his desire to be nice to Hank at this early
stage of his new career with the firm, he continued to avoid the
kind of healthy confrontation that might have helped resolve the
issue.

## The Motives and Symptoms

The above stories contain apparently good reasons to try to be
nice by avoiding confrontation. Aaron thought it was more important to treat others courteously and patiently and go above and
beyond the call of duty than to be open and honest with them.
And Casey was trying hard to be considerate of his new coworker,
Hank. He didn't want to foster conflict so early in Hank's time
with the company, so he avoided having the kind of assertive conversation that might have created a better foundation for their
work together. He let Hank continue to interrupt and contradict
him in front of clients rather than risk the possibility of uncomfortable conflict.

Once again, well-intentioned motives led nice people to choose
ineffectual behavior that created relationship issues and other

unfortunate consequences for them and their organizations. Aaron's overly nice behavior compromised his restaurant locations by allowing competition to set up shop right next door. And Casey missed opportunities to contribute to Hank's learning and adjustment to the firm by letting Hank's inappropriate behavior go unchecked. Add to that the confusing and ineffectual service their clients were receiving, and we have a potent example of how being overly nice can create some "anything but nice" results. Together these stories clearly exemplify the risks of choosing not to confront when it is most needed, reflecting a central part of the Nice Guy Syndrome.

So what are the symptoms related to nice guy tendencies when avoiding confrontation?

1. *Situational Denial.* Part of the difficulty that overly nice guys have with confronting others when it is really needed is simple denial. They have a tendency to expect that the situation will somehow correct itself. They seem to think that if they are consistently nice and treat others with deference and unquestioning supportive behavior—even when problems arise that need to be confronted—all will be well. Instead, others are not getting honest communication and feedback that may be badly needed. And overly nice guys risk being taken advantage of because of their overniceness.

2. *Fear of Disapproval.* In situations involving potential confrontation, fear of rejection and disapproval can be very powerful. Nice guys seem to fear that if they challenge others, even when real problems emerge that need to be addressed, they will risk disapproval and rejection. They may fear that by confronting others they will not only come across as unreasonable but their working relationships will be irreparably damaged. Perhaps they are ultimately concerned that their relationships will break down and they will consequently fail. Ironically, their desire to be "nice"

and their apparent fear of disapproval set them up for the very disapproval, rejection, and failure they are trying to avoid.

3. *Intimidation.* Certain people and situations can be intimidating to overly nice guys, who are easily bullied by those who speak louder, more forcefully, and more often. They fear the (perceived) power that others wield. Or they become inhibited and fall silent, refusing to confront situations that overwhelm them. They are intimidated by a corporate culture that encourages healthy confrontation and debate, and they personally fear the thought of confronting associates and bringing disagreements to the surface.

Being able to confront others when it is needed is one of the most challenging skills for overly nice guys to learn. To be clear, we are not advocating being unreasonably difficult and confronting everyone on issues in a way that stirs up destructive conflict. Rather, it is the avoidance of confronting real problems between people that naturally emerge and that need to be discussed with openness and honesty that reflects a key symptom of the Nice Guy Syndrome.

Aaron seemed oblivious to this hidden risk. In fact, he saw what may have been healthy dialogue as undesirable behavior that he wished to avoid. Unfortunately, he was contributing to knowledge gaps and insulated thinking and setting himself and others up to miss the potential synergies that can be realized from the healthy confrontation of ideas. Casey, on the other hand, suffered from this shortfall in an even more obvious way by avoiding honest communication with the very person he was in partnership with as he performed his job during every client sales call.

It's no surprise that overly nice people will naturally tend to avoid confrontation, especially if it could result in any temporary discomfort for others. Nevertheless, when they constructively confront issues that clearly need to be addressed, everyone stands to benefit in the long run. While all this can be challenging, there are some nice guy strategies specifically designed to promote success in exercising *the right to confront*.

## NICE GUY STRATEGIES
## Confronting Confrontation

We invite you to change your perception. Confrontation is *not* inherently a bad thing. Instead of regarding it with dread and consternation, we encourage you to embrace it. It's normal. It's natural. It's healthy. Most of all, it's necessary.

In the business world, people have differences of opinion and make choices that cause misunderstandings and disagreement. That's a given. Conflict-filled situations will arise with coworkers, customers, and vendors. Do not be shocked or surprised by this. Expect it. Plan for it. Manage it. You don't just have the right to confront those situations, you have the *responsibility*. The willingness to use confrontation when it is needed is an important key to greater effectiveness. Through the introduction of healthy confrontation (and risking being a bit less "nice" in the short term), nice guys end up being better (and ultimately *nicer*) colleagues to those with whom they work—and better able to serve clients and customers as well.

Successful confrontation requires many skills, including self-awareness, speaking up, setting boundaries, making choices, and being bold—virtually every principle discussed elsewhere in this book. But most of all, it takes courage and honesty. "We talk about fair and firm around here," says Jon Luther of Dunkin' Brands. "We're fair with people, but we're firm about what we want. If you don't enjoy confrontation because you're too nice and you don't want to hurt people's feelings, you can't address tough issues.

That's not about being nice or not being nice. That's a lack of courage. Leaders have to have courage because then they can make the tough calls."

Make dealing with conflict—in a healthy way—a normal part of doing business. It is a skill that can be learned. But first, the problem must be recognized.

## NICE GUY STRATEGY: Recognize

Before a challenging situation can be confronted, one must first admit that a problem exists. Like ostriches with their heads in the sand, overly nice guys often go to great lengths to deny a problem exists. It's Nice Guy Syndrome at its worst, as personified by the symptom of denial. They may know that something is wrong, but an "out of sight, out of mind" mentality allows them to put the issue on the mental back burner, hoping it will eventually rectify itself or go away if they continue to ignore it.

Ignorance is not bliss. Choosing to ignore conflict, avoid confrontation, and have selective "amnesia" will invariably lead to long-term personal and organizational complications that can easily undermine the integrity of a team and an organization.

The following story reflects just such a situation. As a manager, Brian could not continue to ignore a conflict that was festering between two individuals on his team. It had to be confronted.

### The 2,000-Pound Gorilla

Brian led a twelve-person marketing team within a $350 million software company. Patty and Joleen were both talented and dedicated individual contributors in his group. Patty developed marketing programs; Joleen executed those programs and got bids from vendors based upon Patty's creative specs. Hence, they needed to work well together. They didn't. The friction between them was obvious and counterproductive. Each would complain and snipe to coworkers about the other, but they refused to talk directly to each other about the frustrations they were experiencing (or work toward a resolution).

This passive-aggressive behavior was becoming intolerable for Brian. Managing them had become his biggest challenge. He initially coached them to get beyond their differences, have empathy for the other person, and focus on the task at hand. "It became clear that the 'nice' approach wasn't working," he said. "Everyone *knew* that there was this two-thousand-pound gorilla in the room—that they didn't get along—but neither one of them would confront it. And it was becoming toxic."

It was time to confront the gorilla. "Why can't people just admit the obvious?" he wondered. "It was obvious to everyone that they had a problem. Why can't they just own up to it and talk about it?" So Brian asked them both into his office, sat them down, and stated, "You guys aren't getting along. It's obvious, it's really affecting the group's productivity, and it can't continue."

Brian let them know that getting along was a key part of their job descriptions that was not negotiable. He then instructed them to take turns confronting each other and explaining exactly why they were feeling so frustrated. At first they were completely mortified to have to admit these feelings, face-to-face, to the other person. "It was like pulling teeth," recalled Brian. Eventually, they each opened up, however, and found a place of honesty, understanding, and empathy. It was cathartic for both of them. Brian then asked each to offer suggestions to the other on how they could make their job easier. Together they formed a plan for working and communicating in a more efficient and effective way in the future.

Recognition is the first step in successfully managing confrontation. While petty issues can be confronted in a light and humorous way or even ignored, significant problems rarely self-correct or disappear. In fact, they almost always get worse. Brian understood that he needed to get both Patty and Joleen to first admit that there was a problem and then discuss it honestly and directly with the other person. He needed to nip this personality clash in the bud or risk creating a toxic group dynamic.

Confronting difficult situations can also make other people uncomfortable, as Brian experienced with Patty and Joleen. The other party may beg you to delay the confrontation or insist that it's not necessary. And you may gain popularity (temporarily) if you acquiesce. But the irony is that avoiding confrontation is really not *nice* at all—at least not in an authentic way. While on the surface it may seem nice to avoid stirring up the pot and confronting people, at a deeper level it is *much* nicer to do what needs to be done to help your employees be effective and productive. As a manager, is it "nice" to abdicate your responsibilities and set others up to fail? Is it "nice" to avoid uncomfortable issues, let them fester, and allow them to put the productivity and success of the business at risk?

Jim Turley of Ernst & Young remembers a conversation with an employee he managed who had made a mistake in her work. "She comes into my office, sits down, and we talk about it," he recalls. "At the end of it she says, 'You know, Jim, when I screw something up and have to discuss it with you, I learn a lot and also feel good about myself after getting your feedback.' It's having the confidence to give them direct feedback in a constructive way. It is a nice thing to do, it's the respectful thing to do, and, frankly, I think it's the effective thing to do. That's where being nice links with team effectiveness and organizational effectiveness. Being too nice and not delivering that message is just the opposite."

## NICE GUY STRATEGY: Humanize

Fear of disapproval and intimidation are two ways in which Nice Guy Syndrome inhibits overly nice guys from confronting others. How can someone confront another person if he or she is worried about being popular or being dominated? Both situations lead nice guys to give away their power. It skews their perspective since they are more concerned with the interpersonal interaction than with resolving the important issue at hand.

How can a nice guy get beyond this? The situation can be defused and improved if you *humanize* it. To better understand this strategy, we're going to ask you to consider these seemingly paradoxical statements:

*We're all different. We're all the same.*

Allowing these contradictory statements to coexist side by side, and then understanding their deeper meanings, is a powerful strategy for effective conflict resolution.

Let's discuss the first statement: *We're all different.* It's very easy and quite common to fall into the trap of expecting others to act and respond to situations the same ways that we do. We subconsciously assume that our coworkers will feel, speak, and choose just like us. And when they inevitably do *not*, we then assume that their reasons for speaking or choosing otherwise must be the same as the reasons that *we* would speak or choose otherwise (i.e., they're not interested, they're angry, etc.).

It is not productive (and rarely accurate) to make assumptions like these. Why do we make them? How can anyone truly *know* why people behave the way that they do or make the choices that they do unless we talk to them and ask? Anyone who has ever taken one of the major personality tests (such as Myers-Briggs) with a group of coworkers has likely learned that there are *many* significant differences in the ways that people behave in the workplace.

They have different motivations, different working styles, and different ways of responding to situations. Some of us are introverts, others extroverts. Some tend to solve problems in a rational, cerebral way, while others rely on intuition. Some enjoy the open ended processes, while others crave closure. None of these is inherently good or bad, or right or wrong. They are just different. A healthy organization needs the full spectrum of talents and behaviors to thrive. For instance, a group that lacks people who strive for closure would suffer, especially in the accounting department, while the research and marketing groups would be ineffective without employees who excel within the open-ended creative process.

The bottom line: People are better served if they avoid making assumptions and snap judgments about the behavior or actions of others. Instead, try to humanize the situation and remind yourself that everyone is *not* just like you. If you truly strive to understand the different motivations and points of view of your coworkers, it will be *much* easier for you to confront them effectively due to your increased awareness of what may drive them. When you respectfully ask them to explain their point of view and really listen to what they have to say, it helps you turn a confrontation into a productive conversation. It invariably leads to great benefit for yourself, the other person, and your organization.

Jim Turley understands the importance of communication and mutual respect. He believes that a key to success is to create a "culture of respect, including respecting people's differences. Once you respect differences, then you almost surely respect different points of view. And once you respect others' points of view, you listen better because you realize that your ideas don't necessarily have to be the right ones. It's more outcome oriented. You realize that multiple points of view to any kind of problem will only create a better solution."

Turley points out a crucial aspect of successful conflict management: letting go of the need to be "right." We might amend this statement to say: Would you rather be right or would you rather be *effective*? This requires letting go of ego (and the temporary ego strokes that being 'right' provides) and instead embracing a results-driven mind-set. When dealing with confrontation, a wise person who keeps his or her eye on the goal—a successful outcome—will deftly be willing to let go of being "right" (whether real or perceived) if doing so will aid in achieving that outcome.

Nice guys are well equipped to embrace this mind-set, as they tend to be considerate and aware of the feelings and needs of others. This innate sensitivity and empathy can be a real asset when difficult and candid communications are needed. There is great value in being able to size up the other person and understand his or her motivations quickly. When nice guys combine this sensitivity toward others with the courage to assert themselves, they are better able to generate positive outcomes for all parties involved.

Now let's look at the other half of our paradoxical statement: *We're all the same.* When faced with confrontation, overly nice guys often feel intimidated. They imagine that "everyone has it together except me" and assume their problems are different from everyone else's, as if no one else could be going through what they are. This creates a sense of separation between them and other people and often creates a tendency to put others on a pedestal.

It's very difficult to confront a person who's up on a pedestal. Instead, choose to humanize the situation by reminding yourself that we're all essentially the same because we're *all* human. Everyone has challenges in life. As overly nice guys look around the office—be it a staff meeting, the factory floor, or the boardroom—they should remind themselves that they're looking at people who *all* have struggles in various aspects of their lives. While the trials and tribulations of other people are of a different flavor than ours, the fact is we all have the shared experience of being human. This creates a commonality that makes us the same. We are all connected.

Herb Kelleher of Southwest Airlines uses this principle to help build a more collegial atmosphere among employees. "One of the things that makes people feel more comfortable with each other (and makes overly nice guys feel more comfortable in speaking their mind) is getting people to know each other on a personal basis," he says. "And that's one of the reasons that we bring people together from all departments within the company. We make sure that the mechanics have to sit with pilots. The pilots have to sit with flight attendants. The flight attendants have to sit with reservation agents."

As the saying goes, "Everyone puts on their pants one leg at a time." Why should a flight attendant feel intimidated by a pilot, or a corporate worker bee feel anxiety around the CEO? Do they really need to feel intimidated? When a nice guy humanizes the other person and the situation, what follows is empathy and wisdom instead of aggravation and fear. When we make allowances for the humanity in one another and ourselves, confrontation can be effectively transformed into collaboration.

Aaron Spencer of Pizzeria Uno adds, "When contentious situations arise, the use of humor is an excellent tool that can defuse a situation." He goes on to say, "The importance of humanizing a situation, without abusing authority, will be well appreciated by all participants."

Sometimes this is easier said than done. It's challenging to humanize someone—especially a boss—when they're micromanaging and behaving in irrational, pugnacious ways. Archie faced just such a challenge in the following story.

### Managing Up

For more than two decades, Archie has worked for a prominent government organization and progressed up the corporate ladder to a director-level position. After a reorg, he found himself reporting to Rachel, a longtime colleague who was now the COO. In the past (when they were peers), Archie had always gotten along well with her. He respected that she was a high-achieving person and had always appreciated her talent and intelligence. But now that he was reporting to her, Archie was shocked at the shift in her personality and attitude. As a boss, Rachel was an extreme micromanager who behaved like a controlling bully. He had always prided himself on being an affable nice guy who could get along with just about anybody. But Rachel showed little or no respect, humor, or civility, and essentially projected no sense of trust in him or anyone else on his large team of engineers. To make things worse, her communication "skills" consisted of screaming and hurling insults at him several times a day. "She thinks people will goof off unless she yells at them," he said. "It had the opposite effect. Her approach was really demeaning and demotivating."

Confronting a bully is never easy. It would have been easy for Archie to feel trapped by circumstances, play the victim, and demonize his new boss. But Archie chose otherwise. He was wise enough to see beyond Rachel's surface behavior and tried to see her as a human being who, in her own way, was struggling with her new job and responsibilities. He remembered what she was like before the promotion—when she was more likable and accessible. "I know that we both have the shared goals of wanting to get the work done and wanting it to be of the highest quality," he said. "She's so smart and so motivated. But she reminds me of a former superstar athlete who years after retiring from the game tries to coach . . . and finds that they just can't relate to 'normal' players and manage them well." He was also sensitive to the challenges that a woman faces when advancing in management. And while all of these considerations helped him gain empathy and understanding for Rachel (and helped him avoid overreacting to her behavior), ultimately Archie knew that "bottom line, it's about performance. Her poor management skills were getting in the way and starting to have a detrimental impact on my group— and the agency, too."

Rachel's poor management skills had to be addressed. But what could be done? Archie's initial attempts at gently confronting her and giving her feedback were ignored or brusquely dismissed. A firmer, more direct approach caused her to become even more belligerent and shout him down. This was extremely discouraging for Archie, but for everyone's sake he knew that he could not afford to back down from this confrontation. "I've worked too hard to build my career," he said. "I wasn't going to let these circumstances ruin it." But since Rachel was not responding to direct ways of confrontation (i.e., the way he would want to be confronted), he had to think differently. He had to find a new way to confront the situation that took into account her particular mind-set. He decided that he would "manage up."

He had observed that Rachel had great regard for Bill, the CEO (to whom she reported), and always seemed to have good, constructive conversations when he was around. Archie knew that she needed to get feedback from someone else. So he tactfully worked the relationship that he had developed with Bill over the years and informed him of the current situation. He encouraged him to spend time observing Rachel and his team. This would give Bill the firsthand information he'd need to confront her and help her learn to think like a C-level executive instead of getting "in the mud" and micromanaging.

In the words of Henry Wadsworth Longfellow, "In this world a man must either be anvil or hammer." Archie was not interested in continuing to be the anvil to Rachel's hammer. However, he faced a very difficult, complex situation. He knew that her behavior was not appropriate or effective. It needed to be confronted and changed. But he also knew that using a hammer would be dysfunctional and highly damaging. To truly be effective and reach his goal of having a productive engineering team, he would need to confront her in a variety of ways. Ultimately, the best tool was "managing up" to get Rachel the input and mentoring she needed to be effective.

### NICE GUY STRATEGY: Collaboration

One of the biggest barriers that overly nice guys face when dealing with conflict is attachment to outcome. If the other party with whom you are negotiating senses that you're entering the discussion with a cast-in-stone agenda and predetermined outcome already in mind, they'll likely feel defensive, disrespected, and unheard. No one wants to be railroaded.

Instead, try entering a difficult discussion with open ears, an open mind, and a willingness to work together toward a resolution and a win-win scenario. The dynamic feels collaborative instead of adversarial, and a space is created where it's safe to disagree and challenge one another in a positive, constructive way.

This doesn't mean that you cease to look out for your own interests and the best interests of the organization. It means that you need not be held captive by them. When you collaborate, you develop the ability to look *beyond* your own interests and see the bigger picture. A collaborative mind-set helps depersonalize the conflict and remove subjective emotions from the equation, which then makes it easier to channel the discussion toward a mutually successful outcome. "When negotiating a deal, none of it is about emotion. It's not personal," shares Ron Shaich of Panera Bread. This strategy is about not letting your ego or self-worth get tangled up in the process. Instead, stay focused on creating a solution that serves both the company and the needs of everyone involved, including you.

In the following story, two business partners used a collaborative approach to overcome conflict and find common ground between two vastly different working styles.

### Done Fast, Done Right

Jack and Nelson were longtime friends and coworkers who decided to start a new consulting business together. As with any partnership, the more they worked together, the more their respective strengths and weaknesses became apparent to each other. Essentially, Jack was good at getting things done fast, while Nelson was good at getting things done well. Most of the time, these qualities balanced each other nicely. Nelson's commitment to quality ensured that Jack didn't send things out before they were fully cooked, while Jack's drive and ambition pushed Nelson forward and ensured that he didn't spend an excessive amount of time on each project.

One year into their partnership a major project caused a big strain on this dynamic. Eventually, Nelson's thoughtful, deliberate way of working felt like perfectionism and inertia to Jack. Meanwhile, Nelson perceived that Jack's push to get things done quickly was creating work that was sloppy and unprofessional. The stress of the current project flushed these feelings to the surface. While their mutual frustration was no longer hidden, their shared tendency to be overly nice guys led them to avoid direct confrontation, along with the difficult discussions that would be necessary.

The situation finally came to a head as the pressure and stakes grew to the point where an honest and direct dialogue could no longer be avoided. Because they both valued the business and each other's friendship, they decided to take a somewhat novel approach. Instead of starting the discussion by focusing on their differences, they instead decided to enter the process by explaining their perception of the other's concerns and to do so with an open mind—admitting to their shared frustration, but also making a commitment to work together to find a solution—all while remaining as honest and self-aware as possible.

It wasn't easy. Certain comments and discussion points were difficult for the other person to hear. Yet the shared commitment to collaborate on the solution (instead of having it imposed by one person upon the other) worked wonders. Once they waded through the difficult waters, they were able to find firm ground—common ground—because of their shared goals and mission. They were then able to build a new process that played into each of their strengths and minimized their respective weaknesses. It also set the stage for a healthier working relationship in the future.

Instead of a battle waged between two opposing sides, Jack and Nelson created a collaboration that addressed the issues with a mutual desire to find a successful solution. They did their best to set aside their predetermined agendas and judgments, and instead tried to have open minds—which helped them depersonalize the problem and look at it more objectively.

While it certainly helps if both people agree to a collaborative approach toward confrontation, it's not imperative. In many cases, one person can effectively steer the discussion in a positive, constructive direction and keep it on track. He or she can essentially "coach" the other person by utilizing their collaborative skills and avoiding letting it become adversarial. For instance, it can be helpful to begin a difficult confrontation by saying, "We both know that we have a challenge here. I don't know what the solution is, but I'm sure there's a good one out there. Let's work together to find it." Such a statement can help defuse the situation and make the other person feel like he or she has been invited to a conversation instead of a battle.

## NICE GUY WHIPLASH: Confronting

Sometimes people go to the extreme when it comes to confronting. When someone is new at being assertive and going head-to-head with someone else, it's not uncommon to go too far in the other direction.

In regard to confrontation, here are a few possible ways in which Nice Guy Whiplash might take form:

1. *Picking Petty Battles.* Someone who is new to confrontation often lacks a sense of discretion and perspective. They lack a sense of the scale and relative importance of an issue and can "make a mountain out of molehill." Instead of wisely "picking their battles," they generate confrontations over issues that are petty and trivial. This can ruin good feelings within a group, damage trust, and create adversarial relationships.

2. *Melodrama.* Start with pettiness, mix it with excess emotion and drama, and you get a toxic, melodramatic cocktail of Nice Guy Whiplash that can be exhausting to all who get sucked into its gravitational pull. The practitioner is so filled with self-importance and ego that he or she loses the ability to see the forest through the trees. It often becomes personal as confrontations become soap operas. Gossip and backstabbing can be unfortunate by-products.

3. *Bullheadedness.* When someone doesn't know how to flex their raw, untrained confrontation muscles properly, the execution can be sloppy—like a bull in a china shop, they can run over people with little or no concern for ramifications. The goal? To exert power, or maybe even to exorcise past demons and make right the slights of the past (real or imagined) as a former doormat makes up for lost time. The result? He or she becomes a bully.

## NICE COMPANY STRATEGIES
# Confrontation As a Growth Mechanism

Wise companies understand that confrontation is healthy and that it is the confrontation *experience* that creates a negative residue. When you improve the process and "wipe away" the residue, overly nice guys will be much more accepting of confrontation. Through an organization's leadership, that experience can be shaped and promoted as "healthy confrontation." This approach can reduce unnecessary and unproductive cycles and allow employees to deliberate important issues freely and efficiently.

When confrontation strategies are not properly shaped, organizations risk drifting toward mediocrity. Divergent viewpoints are often minimized, scorned, squelched, or ignored altogether. If ideas are the focus instead of egos, energy can then be spent on nurturing those ideas instead of political infighting or confrontation avoidance.

There is an outdated mentality with some businesspeople who see confrontation as a power play. These people might say, "If people can't confront a tough situation, too bad! They just don't have what it takes." In many cases, these leaders are oblivious to their cultures, where the atmosphere is charged with inappropriate levels of caution and negativity. But it is the only environment they know.

A wise businessperson evolves, developing a greater appreciation for divergent viewpoints and readily welcoming healthy confrontation. Companies are best served when they recognize the importance of confrontation strategies for employees—especially overly nice guys. Because of their aversion to confrontation, overly nice guys let conflict go unresolved, which damages productivity, creativity, and interpersonal relations. When organizations provide the right tools to develop the requisite courage and honesty, overly nice guys become more capable of healthy confrontation.

## NICE COMPANY STRATEGY: The Corporate Tool Belt

Joe McGuire of Tweeter Home Entertainment Group, recognizes the impact of helping overly nice guys achieve more success. From his vantage point, confrontation is a necessity. Providing overly nice guys with the right tools helps them deal with conflict and grow in significant ways. "Everyone has a tool belt to deal with situations as they make their way through business and life," he says. "Unfortunately, most overly nice guys have only one tool in their belt—and that is the 'hug.' While the hug is an important and valuable tool, it needs to be supplemented by others, such as a 'hammer,' 'glue,' and more. The more tools they have, the better nice guys can cope with a wider variety of circumstances by being more balanced and more effective. Good leaders are those who arm their people with the right tools."

**JOE MCGUIRE**
**FORMER CEO,**
**TWEETER HOME**
**ENTERTAINMENT GROUP**

Unfortunately, most overly nice guys have only one tool in their belt—and that is the "hug."

McGuire once had a senior manager—we'll call him "Sam"—who had been with Tweeter for a long time and was recognized as a brilliant contributor and manager. He was also recognized as an overly nice guy who couldn't say no. Thankfully, many of his people had also been with him for a long time and didn't require much guidance. Sam had always done well using the only tool he had—the hug. When challenges arose, he guided them as he thought best—with kind words and a lot of assistance. While this worked well for his senior team, it was not effective for his junior staff. In their case, they needed a different tool—the hammer. They needed to be confronted and given honest and direct feedback.

McGuire recognized Sam's struggles and met with him to discuss the situation. Sam felt a number of his employees needed improvement in several areas, but he didn't want to hurt their feelings. McGuire asked Sam if he believed it was important to be honest. Sam answered, "Yes, of course!" He went on to explain to Sam that he was actually *hindering* their growth by not directly and honestly confronting them (i.e., with the hammer). With some additional guidance, Sam developed the necessary courage and ability to have honest confrontations with the junior team—a step that helped everyone involved, including Sam.

For overly nice guys, the tool belt concept delineates between the person (i.e., the overly nice guy) and the tool selected for use. The overly nice guy always remains nice, and it is the tool that assumes "the burden" for the healthy confrontation. As time progresses, overly nice guys will realize that their *niceness* combined with the *right* tool will allow them to become *effectively nice*. Here are some things to keep in mind when developing a Corporate Tool Belt to help overly nice guys with confrontation:

1. *The Right Tool?* Companies can help overly nice guys by introducing an assortment of tools to contend with different situations and different people. Beyond the hug and the hammer, there are times when you'll need to introduce tools like road maps, scissors, yardsticks, tissues, voting ballots, and a host of others that can make a difference. The tools that you introduce need to be supportive of your culture and style of management.

2. *Unused Tools.* Once you introduce a new tool to overly nice guys in your organization, you need to ensure that they find the courage to use it. A hammer does no good if it sits in their belts without ever being used. They can gain courage and overcome

their fear of using the tool with training, ongoing guidance, and observing others using the tool.

3. *Value-Aligned Tools.* The use of the tools must align with the core values of a nice guy to have meaningful impact. If they don't see how the tools relate to their beliefs, there is a high likelihood that the new tools will be ineffective or ignored. McGuire points out that "overly nice guys will begin to use new tools only when their core values exceed the fear that they have in using the tool." For example, if they saw a subordinate being verbally harassed by a coworker in an abusive way, they would likely summon the courage to use their "hammer" and defend that person if their core values reflected a strong aversion to abusive behavior.

Confrontation can be a vehicle for growth—as long as people do it respectfully and nicely. When the right tool is used from the Corporate Tool Belt, it will allow overly nice guys to deal with confrontation effectively. By establishing a culture that embraces the importance of confrontation and then links it to important core values, organizations can significantly help overly nice guys. With the right tools, they can develop the ability to address even the most difficult confrontations.

### NICE COMPANY STRATEGY: Race to the Conflict

Once overly nice guys are armed with the right tools, a mind-set must be established that accelerates the desire to confront people quickly and nicely, come to a productive conclusion, and move on. It's easy to go to Home Depot and buy every tool on the shelf. However, if you don't use the tool and do the work, the project is never started—let alone completed.

Brian Scudamore of 1-800-GOT-JUNK? knows that confrontation is a part of doing business. "The quicker people address an issue," he

says, "the quicker they can become
more productive." Given its importance,
he has introduced a philosophy he calls
"Race to the Conflict." It is one of several governing philosophies (called
"Rules of the Road") that are taught to
his employees as a way of doing business. Race to the Conflict teaches that
conflict should be pushed to the surface
and addressed quickly and efficiently. At GOT-JUNK, resolving conflict and achieving the desired outcome are highly valued.

In support of the program, it is important that people approach
others with total respect and courtesy at all times during the process.
Business confrontations should never be angry, vulgar, or abusive.
Scudamore recognizes the importance of establishing a work environment that embraces the Race to the Conflict mind-set. By making
this philosophy an integral part of his corporate culture, he's helped
create a mind-set where employees don't just accept confrontation,
they *pursue* it. This can be a transformative experience for overly nice
guys, who tend to go to great lengths to avoid confrontation.

Here are three techniques that support a Race to the Conflict
mind-set and will help blend this approach into your organization's culture:

1. *Reciprocal Listening.* When participating in a confrontation,
it is critical that people treat each other with respect. One must
also take the time to truly *listen* to the other person rather than
begin mental preparations in his or her head for another counter-
point. If one person dominates the discussion, success is unlikely.
It is crucial that both (or multiple) parties participate and are
fully heard. As part of this technique, it may be appropriate to set
time limits for each party involved in the discussion.

2. *Avoiding the Sidestep and the Tangent.* Avoid doing "the Side-

step" and "the Tangent," and insist that overly nice guys deal with issues directly. Overly nice guys tend to sidestep the realities of an issue or go off on tangents to avoid being candid and addressing problems directly. As a result, they often waste time and steer the discussion in a meaningless and inappropriate direction.

3. *Accurate Aim.* If overly nice guys have an issue with someone, coach them to address the issue directly with that person *first* instead of wasting time and energy discussing it with other people. They may need some assistance in preparing their approach for a confrontation. Provide them with guidance on how to think through the issue and communicate it. The goal is to eliminate back-channel gossip and hostilities that can spin a conflict out of control.

At GOT-JUNK, the leadership team embraces these rules and drives the message out to the rest of the company. By establishing a culture where conflict is embraced in a healthy and professional way, the stage is set for employees (and the company) to be more efficient, productive, and successful.

The reality of the business world is that difficult issues need to be discussed and challenges confronted. When organizations provide their overly nice guys with a Corporate Tool Belt and guidance on how to Race to the Conflict, they help them break down barriers and transform confrontation into a vehicle for effective communication and enhanced productivity.

## Chapter Summary

### NICE GUY MOTIVES AND SYMPTOMS

**Denial**   Overly nice guys have a tendency to expect that a situation will somehow correct itself, and when they do, they are experiencing a form of denial.

**Fear of**        In situations involving potential confrontation,
**Disapproval**    fear of rejection and disapproval can be very
                   powerful.

**Intimidation**   Certain people and situations can be intimidat-
                   ing to overly nice guys, who are easily bullied by
                   those who speak louder, more forcefully, and
                   more often.

### NICE GUY STRATEGIES

**Recognize**      Before you can confront a problem, you must first
                   admit that the problem exists.

**Humanize**       Conflict can be addressed more effectively when
                   we more fully understand the commonality that
                   binds us and embrace the differences that make
                   each of us unique.

**Collaboration**  Enter difficult discussions with open ears, an
                   open mind, and a willingness to work together
                   toward a win-win scenario.

### NICE COMPANY STRATEGIES

**The Corporate**  Provide overly nice guys in your company with a
**Tool Belt**      collection of tools to help them deal with con-
                   frontation more effectively. Get them beyond
                   "the hug," as it does have strength, but only when
                   complemented by other tools.

**Race to the**    Instill a culture in your organization that stresses
**Conflict**       the importance of honest and immediate discus-
                   sions when resolving an issue. Then reinforce
                   that perspective by driving people to race to con-
                   flicts accordingly.

## CHAPTER 5

YOU HAVE THE RIGHT TO:

# Choose

MAKE CHOICES
WITHOUT
GUILT

> "Wherever you see a successful business,
> someone once made a courageous decision."
> —*Peter Drucker, management pioneer*

## NICE GUY SYNDROME

# To Be Effective, Nice Guys Need to Make Choices without Guilt

Nice Guy Syndrome can have a dramatic effect on a person's ability to make choices.

Healthy decision making requires confidence, wisdom, strength, and good judgment. This process becomes impaired, however, when overly nice guys give away their power to others and deny their own goals and desires. They often fail to choose a path that is in their own best interest or put their own priorities first.

Overly nice guys "lose out" when they give in to the choices made by others and neglect what is important to them. This selfless behavior can lead them down a path of frustration and disappointment. They may perceive their actions as selfless, but their choices likely stem from feelings of unworthiness. Subconsciously, they may feel that their needs are less important than the needs of others. As a result, overly nice guys sometimes make choices that they dislike or even resent.

In the short term, they may convince themselves that they are doing a kind and generous thing by not rocking the boat, going with the flow, and giving control of decisions to others. In the long run, however, their choices (or lack thereof) will likely leave them feeling discouraged and empty.

## The Stories

The following two stories are inspired by real events and illustrate some of the "Choose" challenges that overly nice guys face in their careers. The stories are different in context and focus but have some common themes. One concerns a new executive manager with significant budget issues and the other centers on a member of a design team for a process reengineering initiative.

What would *you* do? Would you be able to make the choices that are needed? How would you go about making them? Would you be able to continue to make the difficult choices that would likely arise later? It can be challenging to know what choices are "right" or "wrong," and the consequences of the choices we make (or don't make) can be significant. This is true for overly nice guys as well as for the people who are affected by their choices.

### Proposals in Purgatory

Matthew had been recently appointed division manager (DM) of one of his corporation's most important divisions. He was young for such an important position but his performance record had been very strong in the company. He'd also done a good job at building healthy relationships. He was a nice guy and was considered a good team player. The positive network of relationships he had created had been very helpful, enabling him to receive the support he needed for the promotion.

However, once the initial fanfare had settled down, Matthew quickly realized that he faced some very significant decisions in his new role as division manager. In particular, his predecessor had overcommitted to many different projects and now the division budget was constrained, to say the least. In fact, at a time when many new positive opportunities were emerging in the industry, the division had almost no available discretionary resources to undertake new efforts. Since many of Matthew's team members had already submitted a variety of proposals for innovative new ventures, this posed an especially daunting challenge. In fact, one of the first responsibilities that he faced as the new DM was to sort through the proposals and choose what should and should not be funded.

Given his budget constraints, Matthew could support only the most timely and promising proposals. He wanted to be supportive. After all, he was a nice guy—and one of the reasons he had advanced so quickly in his career was because he had established supportive personal relationships with most everyone with whom he worked. But, like it or not, he could not possibly provide funding for every proposal.

Recognizing that the difficult decisions that needed to be made would surely disappoint and perhaps even alienate many people, Matthew became paralyzed. He basically chose to do nothing. Over the next several weeks—which stretched into months—he danced around the new venture proposals issue whenever the topic came up. He tried to reassure the people who inquired that he was giving their proposals serious consideration and hoped to fund them, but in actuality he chose no specific projects to fund. He just couldn't bring himself to say yes to some proposed efforts when he knew it would mean saying no to others.

In the end, Matthew succeeded in frustrating everyone. They realized that he had no intention of moving ahead on any of the proposed efforts anytime soon. Matthew's desire to be supportive and nice to everyone in an effort to foster positive relationships had created the opposite result. His standing with members of the division quickly dropped. They perceived a leadership vacuum that not only reduced their respect for their new DM but also caused them to develop a dislike for him as a manager. And since no new innovative efforts were moving ahead in the division, it was already becoming clear that the future innovation pipeline in the division was drying up. This soon emerged as an issue of significant concern for senior management.

Ultimately, Matthew's standing as division manager began to come into question, and even his position with the firm was in jeopardy. His desire to be nice had made it nearly impossible for him to make hard choices, and being able to choose was exactly what everyone needed from their new DM.

### Facilitation Vacillation

Erica was a midlevel manager in a large corporation. Her company was well regarded for its long history of innovative products and services. Unfortunately, some bureaucratic tendencies had begun to creep into the management structure. To counteract this tendency, senior management encouraged its various divisions within the company to pursue innovative changes within their respective units.

As part of this effort toward creative change, a design team consisting of a cross section of managers in Erica's division was pulled together to consider reengineering their key business processes. Currently, a traditional structure was in place. People from various functional specialties (marketing, engineering, financial control, etc.) were grouped with people of the same specialty. Senior management had asked the design team to consider changes, such as moving to a structure based on product and service offerings, geographical regions, or clients served—or perhaps choosing to stay with the functional design structure but with recommendations for improvements.

Erica was the designated team leader. She managed the group on a highly participative basis but rarely shared her own views and opinions. This worked well for fostering a free-flowing discussion where all eight members of the team actively engaged with one another. When the deliberations seemed to be moving toward a design decision, Erica would encourage members who she thought might have opposing views to speak up and share their thinking. While this was helpful for attaining balanced input from all involved, it tended to keep the group from agreeing on concrete choices regarding a specific design. And while Erica had some definite opinions about what design features made the most sense to her (and seemed to reflect the majority opinion of the team), she didn't voice these views.

She had been told by senior management that her role as team leader would likely require her to make some clear choices to help the group reach an overall decision. Despite this instruction, she felt uncomfortable with the idea of choosing a direction. She was more concerned about giving the talking stick to all members and making sure they knew their opinions were valued and respected.

The design team worked as a group for nearly three months. While the members worked well together and generated many constructive ideas, they had not yet reached consensus on a proposed new design. This was beginning to concern upper management, since they had asked the team to try to complete their work within a two-month period. Consequently, they sent Stan Reynolds, a senior manager who had been with the company for about twenty years, to join the group until the work was done.

At first, Stan mostly observed the design team. From time to time, he reminded the members of the need to wrap things up.

However, after a week of watching the back-and-forth discussions (and Erica's facilitation of balanced participation with little emphasis on reaching concrete decisions), Stan finally got impatient and essentially took charge of the group. "Given the divergent views on all this, perhaps we should just stick with the functional design," he said during one of the sessions. "Is there anyone who disagrees with this strategy?" he asked.

None of the team members—now mostly frowning and squirming uncomfortably in their chairs—said a word. Nevertheless, Erica knew, based on the initial conversations the group had in its very first meetings, that this was the one option that the team did not want to pursue. She could see that the team members were *not* pleased with this direction but were not speaking up because they didn't want to disagree with a senior manager. "Well, it appears we have a decision, then," Stan continued. "We'll stick with the functional design. And perhaps over the coming weeks, you can set up a suggestion box to receive input on some ways to improve the system over time."

## The Motives and Symptoms

In both of these situations, it is understandable why the individuals involved avoided making choices in the spirit of "being nice." In Matthew's case, he wanted to avoid giving bad news to anyone. As a result, he made no choices as to what he would fund with his limited budget. Erica wanted to make sure everyone had a say in the new system design process. She had definite views about better alternatives and what the majority seemed to think was best, but in her desire to be inclusive she avoided making choices to keep from having viewpoints that did not receive group support. In both cases, not choosing a course of action left a leadership void that caused delays and frustrations for all involved.

Avoiding decisions is yet another way that overly nice people can become ineffective and have a negative impact on those they want to support and help. By not choosing, Matthew is unintentionally making the choice to reject all pending project proposals for his division. In his effort to not leave out anyone who has proposed a new initiative, he is in effect leaving *everyone* out. And by not encouraging any decision in her leadership of the group, Erica caused her design team to have little or no say about the future work system design. Her refusal to make a choice resulted in no one on her team having a choice. Both of these situations are indicative of how not choosing in an attempt to be "nice" is a central part of the Nice Guy Syndrome.

What are the symptoms related to nice guy tendencies to avoid making a choice? There are several—with related emotions and behaviors. Here we will focus on three especially notable ones.

1. *Analysis Paralysis.* This symptom reflects one of the most difficult aspects of the Nice Guy Syndrome. When people defer making a decision in the spirit of endless analysis of available data, a kind of mental paralysis can set in. Overly nice people often have a tendency to gather and review data endlessly, leading to postponements and delays. As a result, crucial decisions are avoided, progress is not made, and commitments are not honored until it is too late—if at all.

2. *Deferring to Others.* Overly nice guys tend to avoid making decisions and allow others to have the primary say. They cannot bring themselves to say yes or no to anyone because they realize this would necessitate disagreeing with others who might have an opposing view. Ultimately, this removes their ability to make meaningful choices and instead surrenders the decision-making power to the circumstances surrounding the situation. They think they are being diplomatic and "nice" by not rejecting any options, but instead they actually allow natural forces and external influences make the decisions for everyone.

3. *Emotional Servitude.* Overly nice guys may sincerely want to be supportive of others. However, much of this desire seems to be the result of avoidance of potentially uncomfortable emotions for themselves and those they are leading. They don't want to have anyone feel that they are being left out, rejected, or ignored. Ironically, this can result in everyone involved eventually being adversely affected by emotional discomfort. They essentially abdicate their power to emotional avoidance and to a clock that runs out before any decision is made.

In an effort to avoid discouraging others and to be nice to everyone involved when tough decisions need to be made, overly nice guys tend to avoid making a choice. Matthew didn't want to tell any member of his group that his or her proposed projects would not be supported, so he ended up not supporting anyone and discouraging everyone. Erica went out of her way to recognize every point of view and to keep her team from reaching consensus. Unfortunately, the old saying "You can't please everyone" is true, and her refusal to make a decision resulted in her team's surrendering their power to help make the best choice.

This is a common challenge for nice guys. They resist making the difficult choices that don't yield "nice" results for everyone. But, once again, the end result turns out to be anything but nice for all those affected. Nice guys often find it difficult to understand that by acting in the short term in ways that don't seem as "nice" (making tough choices that not everyone will be pleased with), it can actually end up being nicer in the long run when they're making the conscientious decision that's courageous and wise. The next section offers some nice guy strategies that can help overly nice people learn to choose.

## NICE GUY STRATEGIES
# Choose Consciously and Wisely

Starting at an early age, our parents typically counseled us to "make good choices." They were alluding to obvious issues, such as eating well, staying safe, getting good grades, avoiding drugs, and choosing nice friends. They probably also added a few more words of wisdom along the lines of "Play nice," "Be a nice boy [or girl]," and "If you can't say something nice, don't say anything at all."

Did your parents ever warn you about the danger of being *too* nice in your choices? That we might do ourselves (and others) a disservice if we give away our power in the quest to please others and not offend?

Choice = power. This can be a daunting concept for the overly nice guy, especially in a business context. Each choice is a decision point that dictates future direction and possible outcomes. Our choices will impact our lives and have ramifications on many things, such as the people we meet, the events we attend, the money we spend, the opportunities we pursue, and the success we achieve. Our choices ultimately define the path we follow. And when we are entrusted with making choices in the course of doing our jobs, these decisions can have a far-reaching impact on the companies we represent and the customers we serve.

Some choices are a privilege. Others are an obligation. But they require that a decision be made—*yes* or *no, A* or *B, this* or *that, him* or *her.* And because only one thing is usually chosen, the rest are seemingly rejected. For overly nice guys, this can be troublesome. They find it distasteful or unkind to reject anyone or anything. They strive to avoid situations where they might displease anyone—and in turn have someone be displeased with them. It's to their detriment that they often see life (and business) as a popularity contest. Nice guys need to learn that authentic success is measured by qualities such as effectiveness, respect, and profitability, not fleeting moments of superficial "popularity."

Effective nice guys consciously choose what they will do and won't do. In this chapter, we provide key insights for creating conditions that support balanced choices—choices that help to yield positive outcomes for overly nice guys and the organizations they serve.

### NICE GUY STRATEGY: Ownership

It starts with ownership. It's amazing how overly nice guys often feel like they don't even *have* a choice. "Stuff happens," or "It just wasn't meant to be," they'll say, frequently feeling like victims of circumstance. They're never fully in control of their own destiny or their lives as they give away their power and let others make decisions for them. In the wise words of our former first lady Martha Washington, "I have learned from experience that the greater part of our happiness or misery depends on our dispositions and not on our circumstances."

In other words, it's our *perspective*—i.e., how we *choose* to see a situation—that makes the difference. It's important to know that we always have choices, even if we're not completely conscious of what they are. The skill is to learn to recognize them, claim them, own them, and take responsibility for them.

Can overly nice guys make good choices in business when faced with difficult decisions? What is their initial instinct when presented with a request that requires a choice—asking for time, money, or support? Are they quick to say yes? What's their gut reaction? Overly nice guys rarely trust their ability to make decisions "from the gut" due to a lack of confidence and courage. Their tendency to be overaccommodating often leads to overly selfless behavior and an ongoing struggle to put their own priorities first.

How can overly nice guys break this pattern, own their choices, not play the victim, and keep their power? It can be very challenging, as the following story illustrates.

### Choosing a New View

For more than eight years, Robin was senior vice president of public relations at a regional bank in the Southwest. She was well respected within the bank and the community, and this was reflected in a steady flow of promotions, stellar reviews, and pay raises. When the bank president (and her longtime boss) relinquished his position to serve on the corporate board, the bank's number two man—Bud—became her new boss.

One day, less than two months after becoming president, Bud asked Robin to stop by his office for a meeting. She thought they'd be discussing the latest PR initiative. Instead, Bud blindsided her with a surprise performance review. It was a surprise not only because she hadn't been forewarned but also because she wasn't scheduled to have a review for another six months. Bud then proceeded to inform her that her performance was "not where it should be." He gave her low marks in numerous categories— categories where Robin had consistently garnered high marks in previous reviews—categories where he really wasn't yet qualified to evaluate her, given his brief time as her boss. He also demoted her and encouraged her to "take the rest of the day off, go home, and give it some thought."

Robin was completely dumbfounded by this review and the negative, irrational feedback it contained. While she was stunned and hurt, she instinctively knew that the choices she was about to make would have a big impact on her career. "I decided that I wasn't going to allow myself to feel victimized by this," she remembered. In that moment, she made a choice. "I told myself, 'I'm *not* going home. I have a job to do.' So I went right back to work."

At the end of the day Robin went home, set aside her bruised ego, took stock of the situation, and tried to evaluate her choices objectively. "I know I'm not perfect—nobody is—and I'm pretty good at taking responsibility for my shortcomings," she said, "but I knew that Bud's evaluation was not reasonable or valid. Clearly, Bud was trying to make it so uncomfortable for me that I would leave. I didn't know exactly why, but I could basically see it for what it was—a personality conflict."

Whatever Bud's reasons were, Robin knew that she needed to resist the inclination to focus on him—which would diminish her own power and choices. Instead, she needed to focus on herself. What did *she* want to do? What were *her* choices? "I could have followed my first instinct and said, 'Screw you! I quit!' " she said. "But I'm not a quitter. I could have gone to a labor lawyer and tried to fight it on legal grounds, but that didn't seem like an appealing or productive choice. I could have gone to my old boss—who was now on the board—and tried to work it from that angle. But insubordination against the bank president just wasn't my style. Besides, it would only be worth staying if I could create a positive, productive relationship with Bud."

Robin asked herself this question: What would be best for me and for the bank? "The most important choice I made," she continued, "was realizing that I had earned the right to be at that bank and that my time there was not complete. I knew that I was in the right place, but I had to unravel this situation with Bud and learn what was there for me to learn. I knew that there was a lesson hidden somewhere within this mess."

Robin knew that if she wanted to stay, she had to develop the wisdom, savvy, and skill to decipher this personality conflict with Bud and deal with him effectively. She sensed that he was threatened by her and saw her as a part of the previous regime instead of being aligned with him. She had to start proving to him that she was, indeed, on his team.

It was important that Robin did not allow the situation to effectively weaken her position or poison her attitude. Instead, she tackled her job with renewed confidence and vigor. She chose to believe in herself, be humble, and have a thick skin. Moving forward, she began to achieve on an even higher level than ever before. Ultimately, Robin's choices created her opportunities. Over the ensuing months, Bud grew to genuinely appreciate her talent and achievements. He eventually rewarded her with a sterling review along with a promotion, a raise, and a generous bonus.

Robin refused to let the situation defeat her. She took ownership of the problem, ownership of her choices, and ownership of her career. In this case, she looked after her own interests as well as the interests of the bank. She remained aligned with her principles, stayed true to her code of personal conduct, and did what needed to be done to achieve her goals.

"We all want to be liked," says Dr. Tori Haring-Smith of Washington & Jefferson College, "but part of being in the center ring is that not everybody is going to agree with you and think that you made a right decision. As a leader, you are going to get criticized. You must learn to harden yourself sufficiently to accept that criticism, to read the editorial on the local paper saying that you did the 'worst thing ever' and still come back to work the next day."

## NICE GUY STRATEGY: Pausing

Viktor Frankl, the renowned Austrian psychiatrist, Holocaust survivor, and author of the book *Man's Search for Meaning,* understood the power of choice when he wrote, "The last of the human free-doms: to choose one's attitude in any given set of circumstances, to choose one's own way."

Choice=freedom. They are intrinsically intertwined. The American Revolution was fought over this. Taxation without repre-sentation? No, thanks! The colonies refused to be told what they *had* to do. They wanted *choice*. They wanted *options*. In short, they wanted a voice. Having options gives us power, autonomy, and some degree of control. Overly nice guys aren't always aware that they have options unless they've learned to take ownership of their choices.

This skill can be especially difficult for them to employ in challenging situations. If overly nice guys learn nothing else, they need to learn this crucial skill—the ability to PAUSE.

Before eagerly agreeing to a major request, they need to learn that their first option is to PAUSE.

PAUSE . . . and don't be pressured into impulsively saying yes or no. Resist the inclination to comply. Quickly saying yes may please the other person and temporarily make you feel like a hero in their eyes, but it may not be in your best interests—or the best interests of the organization. Take your time before making an important decision. Don't be impetuous and let the word *yes* pass your lips until you are sure that you mean it. "I'm not sure. Let me get back to you on that after I consider it further," is a per-fectly reasonable and acceptable answer in most situations.

PAUSE . . . and remember that a request is simply that—a re-quest. Consider the request from a variety of viewpoints. Be thoughtful and wise before you give your consent. Your choices are for *you* to make. Do it consciously.

PAUSE . . . and consider your options. Consider the ramifica-tions of each option. What are the risks? Are the risks manage-able?

PAUSE . . . and check within to see if you're driven by the desire to make other people happy with your choices. Do you want the approval of others? If you make the choice that's clearly best for you, are you concerned that others will think less of you and be disappointed with you?

PAUSE . . . and, when possible, discuss important decisions with those whom you trust and respect. They'll likely help you discover options and ramifications that would not have occurred to you.

PAUSE . . . and realize that most situations—especially the bigger ones—are almost always resolved by negotiation. Try to define the scope, schedule, staffing, parameters, and conditions in terms that are favorable to you and your company. Don't settle prematurely. Proceed only under terms that are acceptable to you. And be prepared to walk away, if necessary.

PAUSE . . . and ask: What do *I* want? What is in *my* best interest? Is this a good opportunity for me? Is the request in alignment with my own goals, priorities, and responsibilities? Are there any potential conflicts? Is what's being asked of me consistent with my sense of integrity and ethics? Are there any financial, legal, or ethical issues involved? How will saying yes impact my other priorities and commitments? What impact will it have on my daily, weekly, or monthly life?

Most important of all, taking a pause can help overly nice guys break the pattern of instantly acquiescing to the will of others and doing their bidding without a second thought. This doesn't mean that nice guys will always be thrilled with their choices or always get to do exactly as they wish. After all, there are times in the real world when we have to suck it up and do what's necessary—do what needs to be done. But nice guys should always strive to be *aware* that this is the case. Do it consciously and not by default. Retain the power of choice, even in situations where the final decision is not very palatable.

When assessing your options, it is helpful to notice if your choices are aligned with your priorities. If you want to have a happy, prosperous, and successful career, it's important that your priorities are aligned with your passions. Mike learned this in the following story as he created a new career path within one of the world's largest corporations.

### Three Passions

When Mike began working as a designer for Procter & Gamble seven years ago, it was overwhelming at first. "The people I work with are *really* smart and talented," he said. "It was intimidating. I know I'm pretty capable, don't get me wrong, but I intuitively knew that I needed to step up my game and really excel if I was going to cut it." While pursuing training and mentoring, he stumbled upon a technique that helped him make better choices for his career.

"Someone asked me, 'What were you doing at the moment when you were happiest at work?' As I thought about it they quickly added, '*That's* what you should be doing! People doing what they love are happier and more productive.'

"I thought, *Wow!* It was a huge revelation for me. I'd never thought about it that way—letting my passions drive my choices at work."

As part of the exercise, Mike identified his top three professional passions: creativity, scale (i.e., working on projects that have a big impact), and learning. "Once I did that," Mike said, "it really transformed my career and my life. Until you identify your passions, you end up—by default—doing whatever the dominant system around you makes you think you're supposed to do. You're playing everybody else's game. You can't win that way. You have to try to actualize yourself at your highest potential and play to your own unique gifts. If everyone in the company is doing that, then you have mutual shared success."

It led Mike to envision a new career track within the organization—a nontraditional path he calls the "Creative Entrepreneur." It allowed him to generate new product ideas, create opportunities, seek out support, and see them through. "If you can truly utilize your unique gifts, you're delivering the highest value product to the organization *and* you're satisfying your own needs. The payoff can be huge."

In the words of Thomas Merton, acclaimed writer, poet, and social activist, "We must make the choices that enable us to fulfill the deepest capacities of our real selves." Ultimately, we must strive to have integrity with our choices. Once overly nice guys stop giving away their power and play their *own* game instead of everyone else's, the sky is the limit. A whole new world of options and opportunity opens up before them.

## NICE GUY STRATEGY: Conviction

How do you make the right choice? To which voice do you listen? Ultimately, it's the voice within you that matters most—the voice of discernment. Discernment is the means by which we decide what to do and how to do it. Hopefully, our ability to discern is informed by a high level of knowledge, wisdom, and experience. Sometimes we have 100 percent control over our decisions and have the latitude to do whatever we want. At other times, our choices are strongly influenced by other things—company policies and priorities, advice from friends and mentors, legal and ethical constraints, etc. In many cases, we are asked to make decisions on behalf of other people or organizations, so the stakes are raised for our discernment process.

Joe McGuire of Tweeter gives us a glimpse of his decision-making process. "I sit, I listen, and then I provide an assessment. And for some reason, I have the ability to do that and not get people angry with me—perhaps because I just listen to the facts. I'll say, 'Here's the situation. Here are the possible courses of action. Let's make pros and cons for each of them.' And then I'll make a decision. If it's the wrong one, six months from now I'll assess again and make a different choice."

McGuire is obviously confident in his ability to assess options, weigh their merits, process the ramifications, and decide on a course of action. Will the course of action he chooses be the *right* course of action? Who knows? But he's not afraid to make a choice based upon the best available information that's at his disposal. He's not afraid to make a mistake either. And if he does, he'll reassess the situation in six months and make a new choice.

Overly nice guys are sometimes afraid to make tough choices. They fear the ramifications of potentially making the wrong choice; or they fear the ramifications of potentially making the *right* choice (terrified of the unwanted attention, pressure, and success it might bring). This perfectionism and fear can paralyze their ability to make a decision that's sorely needed.

In August 1975, Bruce Springsteen faced such a choice upon finishing the recording of his classic album *Born to Run*. He could not make the choice to call it "done" and wanted to keep tinkering with it. He wasn't sure if it was good enough and, in a moment of panic, threatened to throw the final, mastered disc into a lake. In that moment, Jon Landau (his manager, producer, and friend) told him, "[The album is] done. If you have another idea, it's the first idea for the *next* record. Although the record sounds perfect to me, *right now*, there's a pretty good chance that it's not. There's a pretty good chance that we're going to look back at it and maybe see things in it that, in retrospect, don't seem perfect. But that is life."

Ultimately, nice guys need to use the best available information, have the courage to make their best possible choice, and then have the conviction to follow through.

Be prepared, however, because sometimes the choice will not be popular. Someone will inevitably disagree, be disappointed, or have hurt feelings. And that's okay. It's to be expected. It's not your job to make every single person happy. "I cannot give you a surefire formula for success," says Pulitzer Prize–winning journalist Herbert B. Swope, "but I can give you the formula for failure, which is: Try to please everybody."

Successful nice guys need to develop tough skins. You *can't* please everyone. The business world is not a popularity contest. However, this does not necessitate the abandonment of compassion and consideration. You can always stay true to your values and ethics. But in those moments when you have complete conviction about your decision—those moments when you know you're doing the right thing—resist the tendency to feel like you have to get everyone to *like* the decision—or, by extension, get everyone to like you. "Being overly nice isn't effective leadership," says Jon Luther of Dunkin' Brands. "You can't make tough decisions if you don't want to hurt people's feelings. In my mind, there are times when you need to be an SOB. Pound the message in—because sometimes people need a wake-up call."

There are times when, with a little bit of effort, savvy, and skill, an employer can add a positive spin to a difficult choice, such as in the following story.

### Meat or Potatoes?

For five years, Vern Butler has been the chief information officer for CWCapital, a fast-growing commercial mortgage company with approximately five hundred employees across the United States. Under his watch, an initiative was proposed to build a corporate software system that would manage all documents in addition to automating key business processes. The CEO and many other influential people within the company fully supported this document management initiative and were excited to pursue it.

Vern was chosen to spearhead the effort, as his department would ultimately own the implementation and maintenance effort associated with it. He went through a rigorous vendor assessment process and ultimately landed on one specific vendor. As he got closer to signing a contract, the estimated costs for the document management project—which was originally assigned a $250,000 price tag—ballooned to $400,000 (or higher), due to the identification of a number of important contingencies and variables. While Vern recognized the complexities associated with the implementation and how taxing it would be on the company (and his staff in particular), he was convinced that the new document management system could dramatically improve the company's efficiencies. However, the increase in price triggered the realization that the system was going to be very burdensome from a financial perspective. This was problematic as the project was gaining momentum. In fact, commitments had already been made to the vendor, the organization, and the implementation consultants, and an enthusiastic buzz was building about the project's potential value.

There was an equally loud murmur from some members of executive management that they were not completely sold on the ROI (return on investment) and that recent market downturn might affect cash flow for this type of project. Although Vern knew that these objections could easily be addressed, his people were already hard at work maintaining systems that would help the business stay competitive and, consequently, they were at capacity. His teams made their concerns known to Vern, anticipating that the implementation of a new document management system would severely stretch the intense demands for their time.

While Vern understood the importance of maintaining the

existing systems, the document management system had a very high profile and was eagerly anticipated by many people within the company. Yet, the two projects seemed at odds with each other. He didn't think it was possible to do them both concurrently—let alone do them both well. But saying no to either project would be very unpopular. He was especially concerned about compromising the goodwill and confidence that he had built with the people involved in the document management system. He was really enjoying working with them; the "nice guy" in him felt that he'd be letting them down if he didn't move forward.

As Vern assessed the situation, he ultimately realized that he was going to have to make a tough choice. Was it better to put off the existing system updates or go forward with the document management system? It was an extremely difficult decision, as either choice would prove to be extremely disappointing and unpopular with many people.

Vern took a hard look at the reality of his situation. After careful deliberation, he knew the right thing to do. Ignoring the company's existing systems would impede its ability to produce and analyze key information, and it could compromise its competitive advantage in the market. He decided to push out the document management system for at least six to twelve months so that they could concentrate on getting the core systems updated.

Once he made the decision, he committed to it 100 percent. In a situation like this, he couldn't afford to let people's passions and opinions sway him. He couldn't risk further division and delays. He had to put the business first and make what he believed was the right choice.

Ultimately, business leaders must do what's right for their business—or the business won't survive. Bert Jacobs of *Life is good* remembers overhearing a vendor say, "I know these guys are a lot of fun, but have you ever been in a real business meeting with them? They mean business. They are *in* business. They are not taking no for an answer."

## NICE GUY WHIPLASH: Choose

What happens when someone goes to the extreme in regard to his or her right to choose? What are the possible mistakes and consequences? Here are several ways in which this form of Nice Guy Whiplash can manifest itself:

1. *Selfishness.* It's possible to become obsessed and obstinate about owning your choices. This can lead to a myopic tendency to think that only your needs matter, making you oblivious to how your decisions affect other people.

2. *False Conviction.* If your decisions are based on careless reasoning, faulty data, or a sloppy process, it can lead to dubious conclusions. Basing your choices and your convictions on these conclusions is like drawing a line in quicksand.

3. *The Malcontents.* These folks are choice-making junkies, always thinking the grass must be greener elsewhere if only they could choose differently once again. They lust for change, are rarely happy, and tend to focus on what they *don't* have instead of being grateful for what they *do* have.


# THE NICE COMPANY STRATEGIES
# All Is Not Equal

What happens when an overly nice guy in your organization is so overwhelmed by a decision that he is reluctant to make a choice? What happens when his indecision is costing your organization time and money? You can ignore the issue, you can send him on his way, or you can take steps to provide him with tools that teach him to choose wisely and effectively.

If you choose to ignore the issue, you perpetuate the problem. Overly nice guys will surely continue with their tendencies, such as polling anyone and everyone in order to gain consensus. Or they may spend an inordinate amount of time looking to validate information well past the point of diminishing returns. Or they may avoid making a decision altogether because they lack the courage to make a hard choice.

If, however, you choose to address these issues, your company will become more efficient and the overly nice guys within your organization will evolve into stronger contributors. It starts by first providing them with strategies that teach them how to execute on decisions—what we call the "Decision Framework."

### NICE COMPANY STRATEGY: The Decision Framework

A Decision Framework helps guide employees through the decision-making process. With the framework in hand, choices are weighed against a predetermined series of considerations that help minimize unnecessary deliberation and delays. This process effectively instructs overly nice guys to limit their choices to a specific set of parameters—which helps to accelerate the process. In the absence of these parameters, they are more likely to get consumed with evaluating too many factors, leading to problems like analysis paralysis and being overly deferential to others. When properly armed with a grounded Decision Framework, overly nice guys will get to a decision point much more quickly.

Here is one example of a Decision Framework, consisting of seven considerations against which you can measure and evaluate a given problem:

1. *Magnitude*—Is the potential outcome a big deal or a small one?
2. *Timeliness*—What is the schedule? What are the due dates?
3. *Cultural/Political Climate*—Are there cultural or political issues that come into play?
4. *Compliance*—Are there considerations around mandatory security, health, etc.?
5. *Costs*—What is the financial impact of the decision?
6. *Courage*—What is the right thing to do?
7. *Ramifications*—What happens if we proceed (or do not proceed)?

These considerations are a starting point to help overly nice guys become conscious about *why* and *how* decisions are to be made. The level of formality and the number of considerations associated with this decision process must be reflective of the complexity of the organization, the mix of personalities and skills, and the type of projects undertaken. They will need to be modified to reflect the unique aspects of your business and particular business functions within your organization. For example, if you manage a structural engineering group, employees may choose to perform a more detailed analysis due to safety regulations. On the other hand, if you're responsible for a customer support department, a simpler Decision Framework could aid help-desk representatives in making decisions based upon the financial exposure of an issue.

When introducing a Decision Framework into your organization, there are typically three key steps that must be employed. First, the concept must be introduced and its purpose must be clear. Specifically, it needs to be presented as a vehicle for making better decisions more efficiently. Second, it is helpful when introducing a framework to have already created a sample that's in alignment with your business and business functions. During this process, it's a good idea to collaborate with your people and give them the opportunity to contribute to the content of the framework with which they'll be working. Third, frameworks are an evolutionary tool and require tweaking for optimal use. Periodically reevaluate each framework to ensure that it is effective, useful, and relevant.

When first exposed to the Decision Framework, overly nice guys may be uncomfortable when asked to alter their behavior. After going through the process a number of times, however, their comfort level and confidence will increase and it will hopefully become second nature. Structure is being added to the decision-making process. In the long run, this will free up more time by eliminating unnecessary consternation and decision-making paralysis.

For Jim Turley of Ernst & Young, learning how to make better decisions has been a natural progression. As CEO, he's had the opportunity to lead (or participate in) countless initiatives within his organization. While Turley would genuinely enjoy taking part in many of them, he's learned that in order to maximize his (and Ernst & Young's) success, he must carefully choose where to focus his efforts. "There are a thousand decisions being made around you every day—many of which you would make differently if you were making the decision by yourself," he says. "To me, the sign of effective leadership and effective organizations is to recognize that most of those thousands of decisions don't

**JIM TURLEY**
**CEO, ERNST & YOUNG**

The sign of effective leadership and effective organizations is to recognize that most of those thousands of decisions [being made] don't have significant strategic impact.

have significant strategic impact. Figuring out which three or four are really important is the responsible thing to do. Weigh in on those decisions. But for the others that aren't so important, go ahead and 'be nice'—let someone else guide that decision. This is a sign of being truly nice and respectful. Bad things happen when the person is trying to show that he or she is important by influencing every decision. Guess what? Everyone around him eventually stops making decisions."

Turley essentially creates a Decision Framework for himself by deliberately making his choices based upon his (and his company's) priorities. This helps him avoid getting bogged down in less strategic decisions that don't need his attention or concern.

Sam DiPiazza of PricewaterhouseCoopers stresses the importance of courage in making choices. Establishing a Decision Framework is an important "tool" that can be taken from one's corporate tool belt, as it defines various considerations against which choice should be evaluated. However, if overly nice guys don't have the courage to use these tools (and make the decision), the process breaks down. As DiPiazza puts it, "Once they understand their options and tools, they have to make a choice. Overly nice guys may be reluctant to use a new tool, and overcoming this concern is one of the most critical elements to growth and success."

### NICE COMPANY STRATEGY: Selective Democracy

While business is frequently collaborative, it need not be a democracy. Instead, make it a Selective Democracy. When it comes to making choices, everyone's opinions need *not* be courted or counted—at least not 100 percent of the time. Common sense?

Not to overly nice guys, who tend to assume that broad acceptance is always necessary before making a decision. For some, it may be about making sure that everyone's perspective is taken into account. For others, they may not want to slight anyone or boldly state an opinion that is not liked by everyone. Helping them discern *who* needs to be involved—and *when*—will have a positive impact on their ability to make choices quickly and wisely.

Overly nice guys may need help identifying who must participate in a decision. The following considerations can influence that decision:

1. *Skills*—Does the person have the necessary skills to make a reliable decision?
2. *Input*—Will their input benefit the process and the decision?
3. *Alternative Viewpoints*—Does a potential contributor offer an alternative viewpoint that hasn't already been considered, and, if so, does it matter?
4. *Contributor Count*—How many people are really necessary to make the decision?
5. *Learning Opportunities*—Can other people learn from participating in the decision, and, if so, what is the impact of that learning process?
6. *Politics*—Are political ramifications factored into the participant selection process?

When properly qualified, the right number of participants with the appropriate contributions will expedite the decision more efficiently. The considerations specified are more general and will vary in accordance with your organization's requirements.

On a final note, organizations must develop a culture that can tolerate mistakes. If not, overly nice guys will continue evaluating every possible option and obtaining everyone's feedback for fear of screwing up. By introducing a reasonable tolerance level for mistakes, the overly nice guy's defense mechanisms are relaxed. When mistakes are made, if they are handled constructively, overly nice guys can learn to avoid them in the future while still retaining the confidence to once again make difficult choices.

## Chapter Summary

### NICE GUY MOTIVES AND SYMPTOMS

| | |
|---|---|
| **Analysis Paralysis** | Overly nice guys frequently suffer from trying to analyze every aspect of every situation. This often leaves them in a suspended state of indecision. |
| **Deferring to Others** | Overly nice guys may be unable to express their choices as it might be interpreted as a disagreement with someone else. As a result, they continually defer to others for a decision. |
| **Emotional Servitude** | At times, overly nice guys feel so conflicted about not including everyone else that they become incapable of making decisions. |

### NICE GUY STRATEGIES

| | |
|---|---|
| **Ownership** | Overly nice guys must learn to develop their confidence and courage in order to make decisions. In doing so, they will develop the ability to "own" their choices. |
| **Pausing** | Before jumping forward and agreeing to something, overly nice guys should pause to evaluate whether a choice is correct (for themselves and their organizations). |

| | |
|---|---|
| **Conviction** | Because overly nice guys have a tendency to vacillate for a variety of reasons, they need to make their choices with conviction and move forward. |

### NICE COMPANY STRATEGIES

| | |
|---|---|
| **Decision Frameworks** | Provide a Decision Framework and limit the number of considerations to evaluate when making choices. This will allow the process to move forward. Anticipate that different Decision Frameworks will be necessary for different companies and purposes. |
| **Selective Democracy** | Overly nice guys feel that everyone must get involved in making a decision. They can choose to limit the number of participants in a decision. A Selective Democracy will provide them with the considerations that determine who will participate. |

## CHAPTER 6

YOU HAVE THE RIGHT TO:

# Expect Results

LEARN TO HOLD
OTHERS AND YOURSELF
ACCOUNTABLE

## NICE GUY SYNDROME

# To Be Effective, Nice Guys
# Need to Expect Results

Holding other people accountable for their professional commitments is one of the biggest challenges for overly nice guys. Whether they're coworkers, customers, suppliers, or even bosses, nice guys frequently let them off the hook—or at least soften their expectations—when those individuals promise something and don't deliver.

Accountability takes many forms. It can relate to deliverables (providing what was promised), timing (meeting due dates), quality (meeting necessary standards), or budgets (staying within financial constraints). And there may be a variety of excuses and explanations for the lack of results. Nevertheless, the nice guy often has to pick up the ball that was dropped by someone else or accept work that is subpar, late, or both.

Why do overly nice guys struggle with this?

Maintaining accountability requires the utilization of many skills, including confrontation and speaking up (both of which, as we've already established, are often difficult for overly nice guys).

When you expect results from someone, it may require the un-comfortable task of telling them they're not following through on their commitments or delivering as expected. It often leads to difficult conversations, such as discussing *how* the other person is falling short and *why* they have not delivered—neither of which are pleasant topics for people-pleasing nice guys. Hence, the unfortunate tendency of overly nice guys is to retreat from these exchanges or avoid them altogether—which obviously has a detrimental impact on the nice guy in particular and the organization in general. That's because the business will suffer if high-quality products and services are not delivered—internally and externally—in a timely fashion.

## The Stories

The following two stories were inspired by real events and illustrate a few of the challenges that nice guys face as they strive to hold others (and themselves) accountable for results. The first tells a tale about poor results received by a manager in his personal life that may reflect a typical challenge for him (and for many of the rest of us) in his career as well. The second presents a case about allowing others to let us down at work because of being overly nice.

What would *you* do? Would you expect results in these situations and hold others accountable? How might you go about communicating your expectations to others? Would you be able to assert yourself enough to foster results from others over the long run? Would you be able to do this in a way that others respect and positively respond to? It can be difficult to discern the best approach to take in situations like these, and the ramifications of not setting clear expectations can be significant for the nice guy and everyone else involved.

### When Lemonade Becomes a Lemon

Our first story in this chapter describes an encounter that is very different from the other organizational stories in this book. This event didn't take place in a corporate hallway, a boardroom, or a professional meeting. It reveals something fundamental about how being overly nice can encourage and introduce self-defeating tendencies that can creep into even the remote corners of our personal lives.

James was a recent college graduate who was just beginning to establish a foundation for a successful career in business. He had worked hard to complete his degree and was now a proactive and committed management trainee in the corporation he had joined the previous year. His discipline, hard work, and conscientious attitude all contributed to his being hired into a promising position and he was committed to doing a good job for his boss and his firm. Perhaps naïvely, he assumed that others held the same responsible attitude, regardless of their age and stage in life. Consequently, he tended to accept poor performance from others and to simply let it slide, attributing it to bad luck or unfavorable circumstances as opposed to a lack of commitment or effort.

On this particular day he was returning home from a long day at work. He was tired but content and optimistic about what he was doing with his life and career. He was reviewing the details of his day in his mind when something caught his eye up ahead. It was a young boy, perhaps ten or eleven years old, standing behind a small table with a large full pitcher on it next to a sign that simply said LEMONADE. As his car approached, he noticed the boy's hopeful look. James couldn't resist. He admired the boy's initiative and decided to stop to support this young entrepreneur.

After a brief greeting, James asked in a businesslike tone, "May I have a glass of lemonade, please?" The boy eagerly reached for a glass on the table, filled it with the cloudy yellow liquid, and handed it to his new customer. It was a warm day, so James anticipated the cool sweet taste he was about to enjoy as he lifted the glass to his lips. Soon he had a strange look on his face and gagged slightly. The lemonade was warm and tasted more like sour water than lemonade. It had obviously been watered down and did not have nearly enough sweetener. The boy didn't notice James's reaction. "Do you want another glass?" he asked, reaching for the pitcher again.

Caught off guard, James quickly said, "No, thank you," and returned the still partially full glass to the young boy. "What do I owe you?" he asked, while reaching in his pocket for some change and thinking about the water bottle he had in his car that he planned to use to wash the sour taste from his mouth. He almost fell over when the boy said in a loud, clear voice, "Five dollars." Shocked at the high price, James paid the boy and began to turn to leave. That's when he had the most disturbing realization of all. The boy dumped the remainder of the lemonade that was left in the glass on the ground and then put the glass back on the table, ready to be filled again. He no longer seemed to notice James, instead looking up the road to search for new customers who might be approaching. To his dismay, James realized that there was only one glass on the table and nothing to wash it with.

As he walked to his car James paused twice as he considered returning to the boy to say something. He knew the boy needed to learn more about providing a fair and quality product and service and charging a reasonable price. He knew he needed to be taught something about delivering results in any business situation. In the end, not wanting to cause a fuss or make the boy feel bad, he simply drove away. All the while he realized that a boy only a fraction of his age had taken advantage of him, perhaps intentionally. Even worse, he recognized that others might soon be caught in the same unpleasant and unsanitary trap of the seemingly innocent lemonade stand, all because he had not communicated expectations about better results.

### Nailed-to-the-Cross Trainer

Melissa had already established herself as a committed professional with a track record of top performance. She tried to be a good corporate citizen and do more than her share in the large conglomerate for which she worked. Over time, her reputation throughout her division created more and more requests for her involvement on a variety of projects and initiatives. While this afforded Melissa the opportunity to learn and grow in her job, it also placed considerable demands on her time and energy. Thus, while she tried to avoid turning down significant requests, she realized that she needed to begin requesting that certain conditions be met before she signed on to new efforts.

It was from this frame of mind that she considered a request from Rafael, the corporate training director, to serve as a facilitator of a module in a new leadership development initiative. Given her success at a relatively early stage in her career, Rafael explained that he thought Melissa would serve as a great role model and source of inspiration for the young fast-track managers who were being selected for the training. While flattered, Melissa was at first hesitant to add yet another item to her already very full work plate. She decided that she would request some conditions be met in order for her to be able to participate.

"I am way overcommitted, Rafael, but I do believe this is an important program and I am willing to take this on. However, I hope you don't mind me requesting some conditions under which I do this," Melissa began, in a tone that showed that she was a little embarrassed to ask. "Whatever you need," Rafael responded enthusiastically. "We really want you to be a part of this and can make adjustments so that this can work for you." After apologizing again, Melissa went on to explain why her busy schedule made it necessary for her to ask. By the time she got around to listing some items that she felt were essential—including that she facilitate no more than six sessions, be able to restrict her involvement to no more than one session a week, and have input regarding the training schedule to make sure that her sessions meshed with her other demands—she didn't notice that Rafael had already largely tuned her out. Before they parted, Rafael again repeated how glad he was that Melissa had agreed to be part of the training program.

Over the next couple of weeks, Melissa was heavily involved with her previous commitments and had all but forgotten about her agreement with Rafael. That's when things started going wrong. First she received an e-mail from a senior vice president who was championing this program, thanking her for agreeing to work with Rafael and participating as a key trainer. This opening message was followed by the training schedule. Her jaw dropped as she noted that she was scheduled for seventeen sessions, and in multiple cases two or three times in one week. A number of the sessions also conflicted with previous commitments and with a badly needed vacation that she had set up months earlier. She realized that Rafael had set up the training schedule without ever asking for her input and had not met any of the conditions she had requested when she agreed to get involved.

When she approached Rafael about this he simply explained that when they put the schedule together, they had to consider many factors and the needs of the other facilitators. And when Melissa hinted that she might not be able to lead some of the sessions for which she had been scheduled—or even drop her involvement in the program altogether—Rafael reminded her of the importance of the program to the vice president. He also implied that making contributions like this was really part of her responsibilities as a manager. Melissa was shocked. She realized that Rafael had never intended to make any adjustments to fit Melissa's situation. She felt betrayed. More than that, she recognized that she was going to have to make many alterations to her plans and renegotiate meeting times and deadlines for a variety of commitments she had made with others. She was frustrated and angry, but she said nothing. Over the next few weeks, given her excessive work overload and many scheduling conflicts, her performance suffered, as did her standing in the firm.

## The Motives and Symptoms

There are reasons in both of these situations to avoid establishing clear accountability as a consequence of "being nice." In James's case, his encounter with the lemonade stand reflects the kind of discomfort overly nice people have with communicating their expectations in a way that creates desired results. His intentions were to be supportive of a young boy who seemed to be demonstrating a level of initiative that he admired. The problem was that this budding entrepreneur was apparently more concerned with getting money than with providing a reasonable product or service. Despite some outrageous abuses—such as serving an undrinkable product in a dirty glass and then charging an unreasonable price—James couldn't bring himself to make the boy accountable or communicate even the slightest bit of feedback about his expectations for results. This was no doubt reflective of the difficulty he had in other parts of his life holding people accountable for what they did and didn't deliver. And in this case, other unsuspecting victims were surely going to have a similar unpleasant experience when they, too, came upon this seemingly innocent lemonade stand.

Meanwhile, although Melissa had developed a strong reputation for delivering superior results, she apparently was not prepared to communicate clearly the results she expected from others. Her wish to be a good citizen in her organization frequently motivated her to chip in to help on efforts that were well beyond her normal responsibilities and allowed Rafael to throw her work schedule into turmoil. Her communications with him were not clear and assertive enough to get across her expectations in a way that was both understood and taken seriously. And when the training program was designed, Rafael didn't even consider the issues that were so important to Melissa. In the end, the results that were achieved—a program design that put unreasonable burdens on Melissa's time and energy—were clearly not what she had requested when she agreed to participate as a facilitator.

On the basis of seemingly positive motives, overly nice people can create the conditions for results that are inadequate. Wanting to support others and make contributions that help colleagues and their organizations achieve results is noble. At the same time, if nice people are going to be able to sustain their ability to contribute in worthwhile ways, they need to be able to count on needed results from others. This requires that from the outset they are able and willing to communicate the results they expect assertively and clearly and to hold others accountable for these results. Being unable to communicate expected results effectively and hold others responsible for following through is yet another key part of the Nice Guy Syndrome.

So what are the symptoms related to nice guy tendencies to fail to establish the results they expect? There are several, with a variety of related behaviors and emotions. We will focus on three.

1. *Inaccurate Assumptions.* Overly nice people have a tendency to misread others' motives and intentions. They also tend to *think* others understand what they expect, even when they clearly don't. It's as though overly nice guys expect others to have ESP and to be

able to read their minds. They often assume that what they expect will be taken seriously, even when this is clearly not the case. This misjudgment can leave them vulnerable to unreasonable and unexpected pressures that significantly affect their ability to meet their overall commitments and maintain their performance.

2. *Excessive Leniency.* The idea of "leniency" can sound awfully good, especially to overly nice people. However, *excessive* leniency doesn't hold others accountable for their commitments in a reasonable way, nor does it serve nice people or those with whom they work. Overly nice people have a tendency to simply overlook poor quality, lateness, and broken commitments. They seem to think this is the compassionate thing to do, but it can plant the seeds for others' failure. They avoid providing honest feedback when it might come across as implying even the slightest criticism. And they often fail to confirm what they expect from others in an effort to not seem too demanding. By not assertively and directly communicating the results they expect from others, they essentially invite the formidable pressures and the performance challenges that often get dumped back on them when those others don't follow through as expected.

3. *Aversion to Tough Conversations.* Overly nice guys are loath to confront people and have the tough conversations that are necessary to maintain accountability. Instead of drawing the line and firmly telling others that they are not delivering on the results to which they have committed, they tend to blur the line, move the line, or even erase it altogether—anything to avoid the confrontation that is necessary to clarify expectations and express concerns. Even though healthy confrontation may be exactly what is needed to get important issues out on the table to be dealt with, overly nice guys prefer that anything that might hint at conflict remain covert.

In summary, it can be especially challenging for nice guys to assertively communicate clear expectations about the results they anticipate from others. They often fail to hold others accountable, and sometimes let themselves slide as well. This can lead to undesirable and unintentional consequences. James's prompt payment of the high price and failure to communicate even the slightest sense of the kind of results that were reasonable to expect (drinkable lemonade in a clean glass) were reinforcing incompetent behavior rather than encouraging change. Others would soon have the same sour taste in their mouths, along with the bonus of any germs left in the glass by previous customers. And Melissa's efforts to be a good citizen in her organization were not combined with effective communication of what she needed to contribute to the training program.

It's not surprising that overly nice people have a difficult time communicating what they expect from others and holding them accountable for the results they deliver. After all, they tend to be more concerned with their *own* contributions and how *they* affect others than the results they receive in return. Unfortunately, this sets them up for unpleasant surprises on a regular basis. Fortunately, there are some very useful strategies that can help nice guys more effectively communicate their expectations and receive better results in the future.

## NICE GUY STRATEGIES
# Be Accountable to Others and Yourself

Effective nice guys understand the importance of being accountable for the results to which they've committed—and expecting the same from others. Achieving this often requires them to communicate expectations assertively in a clear and firm way.

"I think people who are too nice often are missing that accountability," says Brian Scudamore, CEO of 1-800-GOT-JUNK?

"Holding someone accountable isn't being mean. Holding someone accountable is leadership. Your followers want, need, and *crave* to be held accountable. They want clear direction, like, 'Hey, tell me when I'm doing a great job, and tell me when I've messed up.'"

Bottom line: You cannot thrive in the business world if you don't hold others and yourself accountable. Accountability takes many forms, including (1) *timeliness*—are deadlines and commitments honored? (2) *quality*—are standards of quality consistently delivered upon? and (3) *integrity*—are legal, fiscal, and ethical standards upheld?

Overly nice guys must define parameters and establish communication channels that ensure accountability for themselves and for others. They can push others to remain accountable without assuming other people's responsibilities when things don't go as planned. This may entail a significant shift from past precedents. However, all participants will ultimately benefit.

### NICE GUY STRATEGY: Expectations

Expectations are the building blocks of progress and accomplishment. It's difficult, if not impossible, for a team of individuals to work together effectively and successfully if they're not communicating with one another about *who* is doing *what* by *when*. And you can't hold people accountable for specific actions and results if they don't have a clear understanding of what is expected of them in the first place. You simply cannot expect your subordinates, coworkers, partners, and vendors to have ESP and read your mind.

To be effective, expectations should meet these conditions:

*Expectations should be defined up front.* From the very beginning, state your expectations to everyone in terms of deliverables, timing, quality, and budget.

*Expectations should be clearly stated.* Clear communication is crucial. Put expectations in writing to clarify and formalize them. If it hasn't been stated, do *not* assume it. Ask good questions to gain clarity on the expectations of others. Making assumptions is *very* dangerous; they are essentially subjective interpretations we create in our own minds of what we assume other people will do and when they will do it.

*Expectations should be achievable.* Objective evaluations of expectations are helpful. Solicit input to ensure that expectations are realistic. Ensure that one person's agenda or working style doesn't inappropriately dominate.

*Expectations should be agreed upon by all parties.* Try to reach a consensus and get buy-in from everyone who is contributing to (or affected by) the process.

*Expectations should be frequently reevaluated.* Conditions change over time as new information comes forward. Don't be a slave to expectations that are outdated, arbitrary, or unfair. Be willing to reevaluate expectations based upon shifting schedules, ethics, quality, and budgets. As part of this process, agree upon some type of schedule that allows for the reevaluation of expectations. Stay focused on effectively reaching the desired goal, and make adjustments to the process when necessary.

Bill Allen of Outback Steakhouse sets the stage in his organization when it comes to expectations, accountability, and results. As a method of demonstrating his commitment to this belief, he regularly publishes his short-term goals for the next thirty, sixty, and ninety days. Additionally, he shares his schedule publicly with everyone in the company so they have a clear understanding of what he is doing. This provides a mechanism to recognize what Allen believes to be most important, and it removes any ambiguity regarding his goals. It also allows everyone to ensure that they are working in alignment with Allen's goals, or else they have the opportunity to challenge them by providing alternative opinions and approaches.

Life and business are not static. Neither are expectations. They often need to be reexamined and reinforced as time passes, or even redefined as conditions change, as Jack shares in the following story.

### Three Strikes

Jack was a C-level IT executive in a health-care company. He knows that there is a strong correlation between accountability and integrity, but there must also be flexibility. "It's rarely black and white," he said. "While you've got to hold people accountable, you also have to adapt to changing circumstances and allow for people's learning and growth, especially in the hospital culture within which I operate." This was in stark contrast with the cutthroat culture of Jack's previous position (within the financial services industry), where he had a hard-nosed boss who once said, "If you want loyalty, get a dog!"

To balance accountability and learning, Jack developed what he calls the "Three Strike Rule." It's a process that allows employees to learn about meeting expectations—with ramifications— while not being so rigid or unfair that you risk losing talented employees. "I had a previous experience where I instantly went from zero to strike three," Jack remembered. "It was so unfair. I was getting great performance reviews saying that I was a superstar, and then *ZIP!* I was gone. I was so confused and disillusioned. I realized I never want to do that to anyone who works for me. Was I clear with my expectations? Is there any way that it's my fault? It's hard to be 100 percent sure about that, so initially I think it's important to give them the benefit of the doubt."

Jack considers a mistake to be a "learning moment." After strike one, what follows is "The Discussion." Jack explained, "In the discussion, we talk about what went right, what went wrong, and what needs to change. I reiterate what's expected of them and make sure that they hear me by asking them to restate it in their own words.

"Strike two is more serious. While I'm willing to give them a mulligan, we have a more serious discussion. At this point we've already had the strike one discussion, so we're on the same wavelength. They already *know* what's expected of them, so there are no excuses. I'm giving them a pass, but I make it clear that it can't happen again," he said.

"Strike three means that we have a serious problem and it's time for serious action. Depending on the severity of the problem, it's probation or termination."

"It's most important," said Jack, "to train your people and set the rules of engagement *up front* with clearly defined roles and responsibilities. The more you do that, the less likely that someone strikes out."

You have to have the wisdom and skill to understand accountability and the guts to hold others accountable for their commitments. Jack's Three Strikes approach essentially formalizes accountability into three phases. It also provides a way for him to hold *himself* accountable for being clear and fair with his employees while also being responsible to the needs of the business. It provides checks and balances and keeps him from letting things leniently drift along without necessary adjustments or ramifications.

Brian Scudamore of 1-800-GOT-JUNK? explains, "Accountability starts with self-accountability. You have the guts to say, 'Did I reach my outcome?' If not, hold yourself accountable. This is about getting the job done—getting the best outcome—and accomplishing it in a very nice way."

Scudamore remembers teaching a direct report how to do a better job of managing others. "She felt like she needed to be harder on people," he recalls. "And that wasn't what I felt needed to be done. You just have to be fair and hold people accountable. It's not about being any *harder* on them. To me, 'harder' implies the 'old school' style. Instead, it's about saying, We've got some rules, this is what is expected of you, and if you don't follow the rules—if you're late too many times, for instance—then it will trigger a chat from myself to make sure that we find a way to fix it."

## NICE GUY STRATEGY: Enforcement

It's not enough to merely set expectations; they must be enforced. One must follow through and ensure that everyone delivers on his or her commitments. Is the schedule being met? If not, what are the reasons? Will a slip in schedule have an impact on project objectives and company goals? If conditions have changed, has the schedule been appropriately reset and properly communicated to everyone involved? What about quality? Are necessary standards of quality being met in all products and services delivered? Is the budget being adhered to? Are business practices meeting the highest legal and ethical standards?

As the process unfolds, it's crucial to have benchmarks along the way that help with enforcement—tracking progress, anticipating bumps in the road, comparing results to expectations, communicating information to the team, and adjusting as needed. Contingency planning is also wise. It helps flesh out possibilities so that if the benchmarks are not favorable, alternate solutions can be proposed.

Everyone needs to be on the same page, move toward the same goals, and follow through on their commitments. It's difficult to be effectively accountable—to yourself and to others—if you are not able to communicate well. It's important that overly nice guys—whether they are managing the team or a team member—are willing to speak up, set boundaries, and confront situations. They must have the courage to give and receive difficult information and risk being perceived as "not nice" when it's in the service of higher goals and priorities.

Another problem with being overly nice is that it's time-consuming. There can be a wonderful efficiency to having the courage to "cut to the chase" instead of beating around the bush for fear of making someone unhappy. "With overly nice behavior, it takes you longer to get there," says Dr. John Seffrin of the American Cancer Society. "And you have to have more feel-good meetings to get people on board. And those are very expensive. You need to have them in any organization—and certainly one like ours—because you often have to build a consensus. But consensus building is not cheap and it's not quick."

Learning to balance consideration for the individual and delivering results to the organization while striving to be "nice" is tricky business. Terry Stinson of Bell Helicopter states, "People have a tendency to mix their priorities up between service to the company versus service to the people. There is a tendency for people to overly fixate on feelings. Sometimes, they need to be reminded that people may like them more—but respect them less—if they continue to act with a sole focus on the people. And respect is more important than popularity."

*Respect is more important than popularity.* This is a huge concept for overly nice guys to grasp and assimilate, given their desire to be liked. There is certainly nothing wrong with being collegial and fraternal, which helps build teamwork and rapport. It just can't be the number one priority in business. It cannot supersede delivering on your commitments and doing what's right for the company, as Kristi learned when she started her new job within a large not-for-profit institution.

### New Kid on the Block

Whenever she started a new job, Kristi's tendency was to take her time before making any significant decisions. She liked to do a lot of listening and learning—giving everyone the benefit of the doubt—before charting a course for the future. So when she started her new job as executive director for a large community action agency, she employed this approach once again. It quickly became apparent, however, that there were accountability issues with Art, her fiscal director. She noticed poor workmanship, unreliable financial information, negligent timelines, and poor staff supervision. Sensing hints of incompetence and (perhaps) sneakiness, she didn't know if she could trust the numbers he provided.

Art's close bond with the previous executive director had provided him with a sense of security and shielded him from being accountable. Recalled Kristi, "They evidently created a management style where they made all decisions together—without any input from the staff—and then simply told them what was going to happen. 'Do as I say' was their motto. It was demoralizing to the staff."

While Kristi didn't want to confront her number two person so soon upon her arrival and tell him that his job was on the line, she realized that she quickly had to do something or she risked losing the respect and confidence of her staff and her board. "In a smaller business, it's easier to get away with softer, 'nice guy' behavior," she said. "But I was now at one of the biggest nonprofits in the state. I could still be nice, but I couldn't and shouldn't ignore his performance. I couldn't sweep a serious problem under the rug. It would not be fair to the organization. I had to be accountable and maintain integrity for myself."

Kristi decided to confront Art by making it clear what she expected from him. She also put him on probation. He was shocked and struggled to grasp the impact of his behavior and decisions. While his behavior did improve incrementally over the ensuing months, Art eventually decided to resign six months later.

To be accountable to herself and her agency, Kristi had to draw the line. She had to clarify standards with Art, define accountability based upon priorities, quality, ethics, and fiscal integrity, and then enforce them. Would it be *authentically* nice to let someone like Art continue in his job? No, it wouldn't. John Pepper, formerly of Proctor & Gamble, relates to this idea. "We used to talk about it in terms of doing the right thing and finding the right balance between respect and consideration for the individual and doing what's right for the organization."

An irony that often escapes overly nice guys is that, in the long run, you're *not* doing an individual any favors by allowing the person to be unaccountable or continue on a project or in a job in which they are not able to perform at a high level. How can you know if this is the case? Ask yourself these questions: Are the expectations of the job clear? Can coaching and/or training likely get them to a level where they can excel in their position? Does the job match their skills? If not, you'll do them a great service by approaching them with integrity and encouraging them to move on to find a project or a job for which they are better suited. It's the ultimate enforcement of accountability.

Southwest Airlines' Herb Kelleher weighs in on the subject: "We have found in many cases that the person who's overly nice is, in effect, oppressing the person who works for them. And what do I mean by that? We find in innumerable instances that somebody who's not performing the job to the standards that we expect is in the wrong job. But because his boss is so nice, the boss doesn't help the person find the right job where he can be a superstar."

Ultimately, the organization won't thrive— or even survive— if employees are not held accountable for excelling in their work. When discussing with journalists whether he would remove struggling pitcher Mike Mussina from the starting rotation, Yankee manager Joe Torre said, "You like to be loyal to your players. But loyalty to all twenty-five comes before loyalty to any individual." If you are not accountable to the success of the team or company, then the company won't continue to exist for long (or, in the case of a baseball team, it will sink into last place).

## NICE GUY STRATEGY: Evaluation

The project is over. The product has been launched, the Web site's gone live, the training module finished, the program written, the deal landed, and the merger completed. Let's wrap it up and move on to the next big thing, right?

Wrong. Now is the perfect time to look back at the process and evaluate the results objectively. Evaluating a project after it's been completed helps define future standards for performance— standards that are more effective because they're based upon real-life experiences. Don't rush ahead and miss the opportunity to learn from the past. Were all of the expectations, projections, and goals realistic? Perform an evaluation based upon quality, timeliness, ethics, and budget. Seek out feedback from your team, superiors, vendors, and, if possible, your customers and clients. Then document the process so that others can benefit from your experience.

Overly nice guys, however, often prefer to bury the past rather than relive it—especially if certain aspects of the process were painful and less than successful. It can be uncomfortable to admit that some things didn't go well—and then discuss them. It can be embarrassing to expose that certain results were not achieved.

But if you want to have high standards and excel as an individual (and an organization), then you must be willing to be honest and learn from your mistakes.

Another step in the evaluation process is to incorporate the lessons learned into future work. People and processes will need to adjust as a result of this input. Making these changes can be uncomfortable for overly nice guys—especially if they have to be the ones to deliver the "bad news." These past lessons, however, provide information, or "data," if you will—typically reviewed and agreed to by a group of people—that can support recommendations for change. Hence, change is not happening because of "one nice guy's opinion" but instead because of a deliberate and objective evaluation and the resulting recommendations.

Evaluating your performance on an ongoing basis is a healthy practice. In addition to learning lessons from the past, it is also important to evaluate yourself against the values and standards that you (and your organization) deem important. Some of these qualities may already be institutionalized as part of a formal performance review process. Others may be issues of a more personal nature—questions that you may want to ask of yourself, such as: Did I meet my commitments? Are there any areas where I could have done a better job of being more accountable to myself (and to others)? Did I deliver value to the company—and did the experience deliver value to me? What were the roadblocks that kept me from reaching my potential? What would I do differently next time? What qualities do I need to embody to take my performance to a higher level? Was the experience in alignment with my career goals? Was I able to uphold my ethical and moral values? Did I enjoy the experience?

In the following story, Mike had to up his game in order to deliver the results that were expected within a very demanding corporate culture—a culture that makes evaluations a rigorous part of the employer-employee relationship.

### Delivering on Expectations

As an employee of Procter & Gamble—a corporate culture that rewards highly motivated people and sidelines the rest—Mike had to learn quickly about accountability. "At P&G, you have the responsibility and freedom to define your own career path," he said. "I find it liberating. The organization wants new ideas, new ways of working more effectively, and to win in the market. It's my job to deliver that. It's a very positive, collaborative culture filled with unbelievably smart, driven people. It's all about building ideas, initiatives, and the business. There's an intense passion for winning."

Each year, P&G does an extensive evaluation of all its employees. They are rigorously measured on goals, accomplishments, leadership, team building, ROI, and contributions to the business. "At a basic level," Mike said, "there is unlimited potential—based on your ability to deliver value back to the organization. The twist is . . . you've *got* to keep delivering bigger and better or you're left behind. Everything is measured against the core principles and how you've delivered on expectations. It always goes back to the business."

"We place enormous emphasis on what we call our Purpose, Principles, and Values," says John Pepper, "and we really talk about them and aim to live them. We have very intensive reviews of performance where you do have to address these issues, especially if the person is not performing satisfactorily. It is important to have values and processes that force one to confront performance issues."

"When hiring people," Pepper adds, "we have many criteria. We try hard to get at those basic character elements of leadership, decisiveness, curiosity, integrity, courage, and innovation. We look for qualities that lead to a person being willing and able to confront issues. We keep striving to learn how we can do all of this better."

### NICE GUY WHIPLASH: Expect Results

What are the behaviors of someone who goes *way* too far in the opposite direction in regard to accountability and expecting results? In other words, what does an accountability freak look like? We've seen a few of them in our day, including:

1. *The Bully.* Using accountability as an excuse to push people around in a mean-spirited way is the sign of a bully. A highly competitive demeanor can lead to hostile, overaggressive tendencies, which usually stem from a lack of self-esteem and a need to pump up one's own ego at the expense of others.

2. *The Fastidious Freak.* This type of person *loves* process and *loves* closure—so it's not uncommon for them to go off the charts on accountability due to an obsessive, fussy, unreasonable, and stubborn nature. Because they are frequently too narrow and lack perspective, they often have too rigid a focus on short-term results at the expense of the big picture. In their compulsive pursuit of crossing their t's, dotting their i's, and checking off boxes on their "To Do" list, they can drive everyone on a team crazy as they lose sight of bigger goals and priorities.

NICE COMPANY STRATEGIES

## Results in the Ranks

When it comes to results—the tangible ones that you can count on and measure—overly nice guys need help. Their willingness to accept ambiguous definitions and assume that everything is understood is problematic. Frequently, they don't think through all aspects of a situation. They also have trouble avoiding pitfalls and planning for contingencies to ensure that the business consistently achieves expected results.

One of the biggest challenges that a manager faces with employees (especially overly nice guys) is ensuring that expectations are clearly *understood* and that they are *realistic*. While company leaders are ultimately responsible for ensuring that this takes place, it is imperative that they systematically teach their people how to work together on their own and without unnecessary managerial intervention. Effective strategies and tools are needed. And because no two employees are exactly the same, these strategies and tools must allow for differing styles, abilities, and experience levels while also providing for a common set of standards and expectations.

### NICE COMPANY STRATEGY: Getting on the Same Page

One significant issue that gets in the way of achieving results within organizations is the tendency of people to frequently have very different interpretations of the same information or situation as they discuss a specific goal. While everyone may agree to a particular set of actions, the interpretation of those actions is highly subjective and is influenced by each person's context. In other words, everyone isn't on the same page (or even in the same chapter!). For this reason, it is imperative that overly

**JEFF TAYLOR**
**FOUNDER AND FORMER CEO, MONSTER.COM;**
**FOUNDER AND CEO, EONS.COM**

In the absence of having a candid discussion . . . you simply cannot obtain clarity on the expected outcome.

nice guys consistently clarify their expectations—and ask others to do the same.

In certain respects, this is similar to the chore of putting away the dishes. Everyone would agree that at some point in their life they have "put away their dishes" after a meal. To some, this means you put your dish in the sink. For others, it means you cleared your plate, washed your dish, and placed it in the dishwasher. And for others, it consists of all of the above plus washing the pots and pans and cleaning up the entire kitchen. And for everyone, if you were asked, "Did you put away the dishes?" your answer would be yes—and you would be right. But each person's unique perception would represent very different results. Unless everyone has a common definition of "putting away the dishes," there is little or no clarity around what actually happened.

When it comes to clarifying the desired results (i.e., clearly articulating *how* the dishes have been put away), "niceness" can get in the way and exacerbate the problem. Overly nice guys rarely push themselves (and others) to ensure that the expectations are well communicated and that progress is properly reported. They are much too willing to take "I understand," "I've got it under control," or "No problem" as acceptable answers. They do not probe further with necessary questions to clarify expectations and enforce accountability. Jeff Taylor of Monster.com and Eons.com says, "In the absence of having a candid discussion—which at times may be painful—you simply cannot obtain clarity on the expected outcome."

This is of course easier said than done. Dr. John Seffrin of the American Cancer Society comments, "There needs to be clear articulation on everyone's part when you're agreeing upon a particular business strategy—to get there and to get results. Is an overly nice guy willing to push back hard and say, 'What about this and how

about that?' And if he or she is *not* willing to have a conversation . . .
that's when being too nice becomes not nice at all."

Without this conversation, the overly nice guy plunges ahead
and focuses on his or her own responsibilities (as he or she understand them to be). However, down the road ambiguity will likely
arise—and the actual results will prove to be much different
from the expected ones.

So how can you help overly nice guys push back in the heat of
battle and hold others (and themselves) accountable? Here are
some specific ways you can help them:

1. *Real Time Collaboration and Action Item Distribution.* When
overly nice guys work together, instruct them to designate a person to record notes that reflect the actions and conclusions of the
meeting. Prior to disbanding, the group should clarify, concur,
and define how they will continue in their respective tasks. If confusion exists, it must be addressed before leaving the meeting.

2. *Did We Hear One Another?* When working with coworkers
on a particular task that has a predefined output or results, it is
very helpful to invest additional time to document your understanding of your tasks and distribute them to other people. This
technique is especially helpful when people gather to discuss a
strategy and the outcome/action items of the meeting are not recorded. When this occurs, it is helpful to have overly nice guys
document their understanding of their respective responsibilities.
In some cases, it is appropriate to ask them to document their understanding of other people's responsibilities as well.

3. *Comparative Examples.* When discussing abstract concepts, it
can lead to misinterpretation and confusion. In these cases, it may
be helpful to provide some type of comparative example of a similar concept or issue that is relevant to the one that is being discussed. For example, if an architectural team is discussing a

particular aspect of a building design, it may be appropriate to introduce a comparative example of a similar building to provide further clarity. This can then be decomposed to identify who is responsible for each respective portion of the task, providing for further clarity and accountability.

When overly nice guys utilize techniques such as these to ensure accountability and deliver results more effectively, companies can avoid the huge costs associated with poor communication.

### NICE COMPANY STRATEGY: What Color Are Your Glasses?

One of the most pleasant characteristics associated with nice guys is their never-ending optimism. When challenges present themselves, their optimism and spirit can carry the day. They excel at making lemonade out of lemons, which is a commendable talent and attitude. However, planning for specific outcomes and expecting specific results requires that optimism be balanced with realism. When a realistic perspective is missing, overly nice guys suffer from wearing "rose-colored glasses," a condition that reduces their ability to see clearly and work effectively.

Overly nice guys have a tendency to assume best-case scenarios without planning for contingencies. In the absence of formalized processes, it is difficult to expect results in a reliable fashion. Even with the best of intentions, rose-colored glasses will skew the process and endanger the ability to achieve the desired results.

For example, overly nice guys may provide updates for an initiative in an inappropriately positive fashion. This may lead to inaccurate and overinflated expectations being set. Alternately, when overly nice guys minimize or ignore project risks, the risks may come back to haunt them. They may refuse to recognize that an "elephant is in the room" and that a problem is lurking. Overly nice guys may also take on too much work for themselves and others, with the unrealistic expectation that the results are achievable.

Joe McGuire of Tweeter Home Entertainment Group had a talented woman on his team who suffered from Nice Guy Syndrome. In her case, she was wearing a pair of *thick* rose-colored glasses—the type that completely prevented her from seeing the giant elephant in the room. In this case, the elephant was an annual review process for her subordinates, all of whom she claimed "had no room for improvement" in their respective performance reviews. McGuire caught wind of this. He asked her to meet with him and bring the reviews.

After going through them together, he probed her further to determine what type of constructive feedback could be provided. In reflecting upon the question, she recognized that there were certain areas that could be addressed. He asked her to score each person according to different criteria and then rank them. She then had to identify how the person ranked as number 6 could improve to a ranking of 3, and so on. At the end of the day, she delivered a much better review. Two months later, she told McGuire about the unbelievable difference the process had made with her team.

When overly nice guys in your organization wear rose-colored glasses, a reality check is needed to ensure that everyone concurs on actions and goals. Only then can they (and other participants) continue toward meaningful results. If this doesn't take place, results will likely be very unpredictable. The following techniques can help address this situation:

1. *Vet the Path, Vet the Results.* Ask the overly nice guy to select a trusted coworker to review the expected results to ensure that they are achievable. As part of this process, make sure that the results *and* the supporting steps are properly vetted. This may

need to take place at numerous times throughout a process to ensure that there is continued clarification and concurrence around the expected results.

2. *Dependency Checkpoints.* Overly nice guys often assume the best possible outcomes from people upon whom they are dependent. When a dependent party states that a task will be completed on a certain day, it is usually taken at face value without scrutiny. This can lead to problems. The overly nice guy needs to learn to scrutinize those dependencies more intensely to fully understand their condition and head off potential problems. For example, if a team member promised to deliver a marketing brochure to your overly nice guy on a particular date, it may be appropriate to put in a checkpoint date beforehand to ensure that the team member is on target. Otherwise, the overly nice guy may assume all is well—until it is too late.

3. *Notching Down Expectations.* To counter the bursts of overly optimistic information that overly nice guys often disseminate, it is best to ask them to notch down the expectations that they share with others. This may be a formal communications program that is used for managing results or a training program that teaches them to minimize overzealous communications (or a combination of both).

> **JACK BOGLE**
> **FOUNDER AND FORMER CEO,**
> **THE VANGUARD GROUP**
>
> There is no company that can trust everything and count nothing. And there is no company that can count everything and trust nothing.

Overly nice guys are well intended in their efforts to achieve results, but because of their overoptimistic outlook and their difficulties with pushing people to be accountable, they need help. Ultimately, effective accountability requires concrete measurement tools as well as trust. According to Jack Bogle of The Vanguard Group, "There is no company that can trust everything and count nothing. And there is no company that can count everything and trust nothing." A balance is needed. Results are best achieved when a corporate culture is built that weaves clear expectations and a focus on accountability into the fabric of the organization.

## Chapter Summary

### NICE GUY MOTIVES AND SYMPTOMS

| | |
|---|---|
| **Inaccurate Assumptions** | Overly nice guys have a tendency to misread other people's intentions. Additionally, they tend to assume that others understand what they mean. When combined, this often results in misaligned expectations. |
| **Excessive Leniency** | Looking the other way when issues arise is a common problem for overly nice guys. Excessive leniency becomes a burden as they inappropriately give breaks to others, because it compromises their ability to deliver agreed-upon results. |
| **Aversion to Tough Conversations** | As part of holding people accountable and expecting results, it will be necessary to have some tough conversations with people. Overly nice guys are challenged in this respect as they struggle with turning the tough conversations into healthy confrontations. |

## NICE GUY STRATEGIES

**Expectations**    Overly nice guys must go through a deliberate process to set expectations and define levels of accountability as they participate on projects and processes.

**Enforcement**    With expectations set, overly nice guys must now summon the necessary courage and skills to ensure that the agreed-upon expectations are being followed and enforced.

**Evaluation**    Overly nice guys must be willing to reflect upon the realities of their efforts by performing evaluations. They must then convert the important observations into meaningful actions that help on future work.

## NICE COMPANY STRATEGIES

**Getting on the Same Page**    Overly nice guys need assistance in properly setting and understanding expectations. In this regard you need to help them get on the same page so that all participants are in agreement with regard to a particular task.

**What Color Are Your Glasses?**    Overly nice guys have a tendency to be too optimistic (wearing rose-colored glasses) for themselves and others. You need to help ground them in ways that allow them to achieve predictable results.

## CHAPTER 7

YOU HAVE THE RIGHT TO:

# Be Bold

REACH BEYOND
YOUR COMFORT
ZONE

> "When you cannot make up your mind which of
> two evenly balanced courses of action you should take—
> choose the bolder."
> —W. J. Slim, British general

## NICE GUY SYNDROME

# The Struggle to Break Out
# of Your Comfort Zone

Overly nice guys prefer to operate within their comfort zone, sticking with what is familiar and what they feel confident that they can handle. They tend to avoid rocking the boat, creating upheaval, or imposing on others.

Why is this so? Overly nice guys are frequently compelled to ensure that every aspect of a situation is explored—in detail—before they will proceed. Or they become paralyzed by perceived risks and limitations—real or imagined—and remain stuck in neutral.

They often lack the confidence to move forward, so their ideas frequently languish and die—if they even get started in the first place. This manifests as delays or inaction.

Finding motivation is an important aspect of taking bolder steps. With thoughtful preparation and assessment, boldness can represent a healthy mind-set that allows for a well-considered stretching of your abilities and comfort zone.

## The Stories

The following two stories are inspired by actual events and illustrate a few of the "be bold" difficulties that nice guys face in the business world. While each story is distinct, together they raise some key challenges that nice people have in making a choice to be bold. The first centers on the career choices of a retail furniture buyer, and the second is taken from the world of investment management.

What would *you* do? What action would you take? Why? Would you play it safe? Or would you choose to be bold? How much risk would you be willing to take to move toward your passion? The choice between taking bold steps versus playing it safe can be very difficult. It's often unclear what the best course is at a given time and in a specific situation. Overly nice guys tend to avoid boldness, and the ramifications can be significant for all involved.

### The Career Couch Potato

Emily was a buyer for Jupiter Furniture, a large retail firm. She was a well-liked member of a buying team of eight people. Her recent evaluations indicated that while she was not an outstanding performer, she was considered conscientious, a hard worker, and someone who got along very well with her coworkers. Emily felt little enthusiasm for her work, but she valued her colleagues and appreciated the decent salary, financial package, and general security that the job afforded her.

Within the past month, it had been announced that two members of the group were making significant career moves. Alberto had received a promotion and was becoming Jupiter's vice president of operations. This move upstairs included not only an attractive salary and other benefits but offered him the opportunity to have a major impact on the future of the company. Justin, on the other hand, had chosen to leave Jupiter to return to graduate school to seek a PhD. This move meant sacrificing his salary and future career opportunities in the furniture retail business and striking out on a whole new career path.

Emily lavished her congratulations on Alberto, but her response to Justin was lukewarm at best. Something about the choice he was making made her surprisingly uncomfortable about her own career situation. Finally, in private, she expressed her feelings a bit more directly. "I really liked college, too, Justin, and I was a good student," she began. "I made the dean's list and my academic department even asked me to assist a new professor in teaching a class. I really enjoyed it and it piqued my interest in getting involved more in corporate training and personnel issues. In fact, I would love to go back to graduate school myself and get my MBA or some other advanced degree. I have dreamed of becoming a human resources executive one day—but I can't imagine taking that kind of risk. What if I failed at the graduate school level? Also, I feel like I would be letting the rest of the buying team down." She punctuated this final statement with a hint of an accusatory stare at Justin, suggesting that she thought his choice to leave Jupiter to go back to school was not the "nice," collegial thing to do.

Over time, Emily watched as various HR positions became available within Jupiter but, in each case, the position announcements indicated that a graduate degree, preferably an MBA, was required. Nevertheless, Emily resisted taking the risk of returning to school to enter a degree program. Then, one day a few years later, she received an e-mail from Justin saying that he was about to finish his graduate program and had already accepted a job offer from a large, prestigious consulting firm. Interestingly, he added, the firm was going to be taking on Jupiter as one of their clients over the next couple of years to help them with their HR function.

### The Detraction of Inaction

Thomas had been a mutual fund manager for his investment firm's "Value Contrarian Fund" for several months. His company relied on a team approach for investment ideas and choices. The managers of the firm's various mutual funds met regularly as a group to discuss their latest investment ideas and thinking about current investment strategies. While each fund was distinct from the others, fund managers often overlapped in philosophy and were encouraged by top management to work together to maximize returns across the various mutual funds.

During one of these meetings, Thomas shared two new investment ideas he had. One involved an out-of-favor high-technology company. It had a strong track record for generating quality products and had earned significant customer loyalty over the years but recently had a couple of key product failures that had hurt current sales considerably. The other investment idea was for the stock of a multifaceted independent power generation company. It had a history of excellent management and innovative performance but had overextended itself internationally, creating downward pressures on current profitability.

While both firms had enjoyed significant success in the past, currently their earnings were markedly down and their stock prices had experienced large price declines. Many investment professionals avoided these stocks because of perceived high risk. Thomas saw the situation very differently. Having studied the companies in detail, he believed they were both laying the foundation for major turnarounds in the coming months and felt the potential rewards of buying them now when they were "on sale" far outweighed the risks.

Nevertheless, when he raised both stocks for the consideration of the fund management team, he met with considerable resistance. One experienced fund manager with a long history in the investment business objected strongly. "You might as well be rolling dice in Vegas," he announced. "Their costs are up, and revenues and earnings are declining sharply. I think both stocks are headed for the dumpster and strongly advise against investing in them."

Since Thomas held considerable respect for this manager and several others who seemed to support his view, he dropped his advocacy for what he thought might be great investment opportunities. He had a large amount of information that he thought could refute their opposition but felt uncomfortable contradicting his senior colleagues. He wanted to be viewed as a good team player and accepted by the group. He also feared the consequences of making a failed decision in terms of a setback for his fund. In the end, he made no investment in either stock, conscious that if he did so—particularly if the investments worked out poorly—the other fund managers might be insulted by his blatant disregard of their advice and begin to question his judgment.

Three months later, when both stocks were up more than 30 percent, one member of the fund manager team pointed this out without noting Thomas's previous recommendation. Thomas, on the other hand, felt painful regret that he had not been bolder in acting to pursue his investment ideas. A year and a half later, when one of the stocks was up more than 500 percent and the other more than 1,000 percent, he began to realize the real cost of his risk avoidance. He knew that had he invested even a relatively small portion of the money he was managing in these two stocks,

it would have put his mutual fund toward the top of all comparable funds in the industry.

## The Motives and Symptoms

Both of these situations contain seemingly good reasons to avoid
being bold, at least in part because of being overly nice. In Emily's
case, she wanted to be loyal to her company and colleagues. She
also wanted to avoid taking risks. As a result, she ended up putting her career dreams aside. Instead, she tried to be a "good sol-
dier" as she marched on ahead in a job that she had little authentic
passion for. And Thomas passed up the opportunity to make what
turned out to be great investments due to a concern that by doing
so he would contradict the views of his more experienced colleagues. He seemed to believe that he would not only be taking
financial risk but also would be coming across as unsupportive of
the other members of his investment team. Consequently, he chose
to be meek rather than bold, at a significant cost to his fund's investors and his own performance status within the firm and his
industry.

While both of these cases were driven by seemingly reasonable
motives, they reflect once again how being *too* nice can create
conditions for ineffectiveness. Emily has embarked on a passion-
less dead-end path that could ultimately result in a midlife crisis
and eventual burnout. Thomas has voluntarily opted for a low-risk
and low-performance approach to selecting investments that could
unnecessarily lead to a mediocre career. In both cases, avoidance
of choosing reasonable boldness placed a drag on the capacities of
nice people to do well for themselves and others. This tendency—
stemming from a fear of failure and disapproval along with a
need for personal short-term comfort—is a telltale sign of the
Nice Guy Syndrome.

What are the symptoms related to nice guy tendencies to resist being bold? We focus on three in particular.

1. *Fear of Failure.* This symptom reflects the core of the overly nice guy's difficulties with being bold and taking risks. When nice people become fixated on potential failure—and the related risks of letting others down and receiving their disapproval—their potential contributions can be greatly limited. They sometimes avoid risking the failure that could come with taking on new challenges in their job or career. In doing so, they miss the chance to gain the opportunity to make more significant contributions and achieve to their highest potential. At other times, they fear possible setbacks that could result from acting on their judgment, even when there is just a minimal amount of risk involved or if they encounter even the slightest opposition from others. They don't seem to realize that their fixation with avoiding failure can actually plant the seeds for mediocrity *and* the long-term failure they are trying to avoid.

2. *Comfort Zone Paralysis.* Overly nice people also have a tendency to get stuck in their comfort zone. They often follow the lead of their peers and avoid entering uncertain and uncomfortable waters. They limit their choices by opting for the normal script of staying in their current job or doing their work in the way they have always done it. They resist venturing into the unknown. They frequently rely on the judgment of others—rather than their own—when they discover new high-potential opportunities that require taking a promising calculated risk. Instead they opt to stay squarely in their comfort zone and the unfortunate mediocrity that goes with it.

3. *Attention Avoidance.* Overly nice guys often avoid drawing attention to themselves, choosing instead to put the focus on others. Bold action tends to draw the spotlight, which can spark hidden insecurity that can be especially difficult for introverted

nice guys. They balk at taking a reasonable risk, even when there seems to be much to gain for the organization and for their own advancement and growth. They go along with the group and avoid the potential attention that goes with choices that stand out from the norm. Instead, they choose to be the "nice" meek colleague who blends in with the dominant way of thinking.

To sum up, choosing to be bold can be particularly difficult for overly nice people. Finding the courage to pursue one's deeper beliefs authentically can be tough. It involves risking failure. It also involves moving out of the comfort zone and facing uncertainty and potential disapproval from others. And it can draw attention in ways that contradict the tendency of overly nice guys to focus more on others than on themselves. Emily's lack of boldness in the spirit of being a good and loyal colleague who fits in with the norm is robbing her of her dreams. And it may well be depriving herself and many others of her fullest potential if she instead pursued her authentic passions. And Thomas's attempts to be respectfully "nice" and fit in instead of making the bold choices he really believes in has cost him, his investors, and his firm the unique performance potential that he has to offer.

Avoidance of being bold is indeed symptomatic of overly nice people. Emily and Thomas are not alone. If they could find it within themselves to risk failure in reasonable ways, to step out of their comfort zone in the spirit of personal development and enhanced performance, and be willing to allow their actions to result in increased attention on themselves, amazing new potential could be unleashed. In the next section, we share some practical strategies that can help nice guys to effectively *be bold*.

## NICE GUY STRATEGIES
# Push the Envelope

People who are too nice are also likely to be too cautious, too timid, and too risk averse—all symptoms of Nice Guy Syndrome (as previously discussed). An aggressive attitude can feel uncomfortable or even reckless to overly nice guys who are prone to focusing on limitations instead of possibilities. They don't see themselves as having the ability—or even the *right*—to be daring and take chances. "Who am *I* to think such big thoughts?" they might say "Who am I to do such a big thing?"

How can a nice guy get beyond these limitations? Boldness is required.

Bold thoughts. Bold goals. Bold ideas. Bold actions. Boldness shakes up the status quo and creates movement and possibilities, and then finds the ways and means to turn those possibilities into realities.

You have the right to be bold. And if you want to excel and succeed at a high level, you have the *responsibility* to be bold. Seek out compelling opportunities, and give yourself the chance to grow and thrive. Give your ideas the chance to see the light of day and be heard by others. Don't diminish yourself and play small. Don't limit yourself and play it "safe."

Many of us were conditioned as children to behave and play nice by our parents. Often, overly nice guys subconsciously bring this mind-set into their adult lives and "behave" in situations that demand courage, change, or even subversion. It doesn't always pay to be cautious.

Being prudent can get in the way. Common sense is often overrated. Yes, overrated, *especially* for overly nice guys. Because frequently the prudent choice—what common sense says is the "correct" course—is *not* the best choice. It is merely the safest, easiest, and most comfortable one. Overly nice guys have the ability to generate bold ideas, yet they often don't act on them.

Significant growth comes when we either push out (or are pushed out) of our comfort zone. To break out of their boxes, overly nice guys must find the motivation and courage to take risks. But fear gets in the way and casts its suffocating spell over any and all possibilities that lie beyond the nice guy's comfort zone. Eleanor Roosevelt, the First Lady to President Franklin D. Roosevelt (who led the country through the dark days of World War II), knew a thing or two about fear. "You gain strength, courage, and confidence by every experience in which you really stop and look fear in the face. . . . Do the thing you think you cannot do."

There is good news in her sentiments. First, she says that when we confront our fears, we *gain* courage and strength. That's encouraging. And then she adds, "Do the thing you think you cannot do." This is a call to action, a call to boldness. Just do it. And then, once you've *done* the thing you "couldn't" do, it ceases to be something that you cannot do, yes? As a result, your confidence grows, allowing you to tackle even more "impossible" possibilities in your life and career.

The bottom line: It is better to aim high and strive to achieve a bold goal than to sit on the sidelines because you're too afraid to try. Yes, if you take a risk, there is a chance you won't reach your goal. You might "fail." But if you don't try at all, it is *guaranteed* that you won't achieve it. In the words of hockey legend Wayne Gretzky, "One hundred percent of the shots you don't take don't go in."

## NICE GUY STRATEGY: Audacity

Audacity is the spark that starts the fire. It's a frame of mind, a way of being. It is also a strategy that you can consciously utilize to help you make a change or achieve a goal—a goal that might seem impossible when you're in your "right" mind.

Who in their right mind would ever try to start a risky new business venture? Who in their right mind would try to invent something that doesn't yet exist, write a first book, or run for president? Sometimes your "right" mind is wrong. Achieving big things requires less caution and more fearlessness. It requires you to be *audacious*—to step up your game and expand your definition of what is possible.

"Audacity, always audacity, still more audacity!" was a favorite quote of General George S. Patton Jr. (who may in turn have been quoting Napoleon). One need not be a battlefield general, however, to be audacious. When Kris Kristofferson—who at the time was a janitor in a Nashville recording studio—wanted Johnny Cash to take him seriously and compelled him to listen to his song (and possibly record it), he landed a helicopter in Cash's backyard, jumped out, and said, "I'm going to *give* this song to you. I don't care *how* I have to do it!" *That's* audacity. It surely got Johnny's attention . . . and the rest is history. Cash's version of Kristofferson's "Sunday Mornin' Comin' Down" was the Country Music Association's Song of the Year in 1970, and Kristofferson's successful career as a songwriter (and later as a performer) was under way.

According to *Webster's New World Dictionary, audacity* means "shameless or brazen boldness." Being shameless and brazen is easier said than done, however. It takes practice to get good at being audacious. The mere thought of going beyond one's comfort zone to consider audacious and "impossible" things can bring up an abundance of fears and perceived limitations for overly nice guys. Perhaps there is no use trying, you say, because you just can't believe in impossible things. What's the point? But some people *are* willing to believe impossible things. As the White Queen bragged to Alice in Lewis Carroll's *Through the Looking-Glass,* "Why, sometimes I've believed as many as *six* impossible things before breakfast!"

Have you ever believed six impossible things before breakfast? Have you ever believed even *one* impossible thing before lunch?! Perhaps you have your eye on becoming a department manager, but achieving it seems impossible for a worker bee like you. Or maybe you've always dreamed of starting your own business but won't allow yourself to seriously consider such a "crazy" notion? Don't repress these desires and hibernate your life away. Instead, give them life by thinking about them intensely; then practice *talking* about them boldly, without shame or apology. "Every revolution was first a thought in one man's mind," according to Ralph Waldo Emerson.

Begin by discussing your dreams and ideas with a trusted friend, spouse, or colleague. Get some energy behind them. It may seem awkward at first, but you must get comfortable with being audacious, talking about your ideas, and *believing* in them. And don't get dragged onto the "Ways and Means Committee" and start worrying about *how* it will happen or *how* you will pay for it. There will be time for that later. Right now, the crucial thing is to have the audacity to *think* the thought, *say* it out loud, and *believe* it will happen. Get enthusiastic and generate movement on behalf of your audacious goals and dreams so that they attract attention and gain momentum.

Start by giving audacity a try in one part of your life. Since it may feel too risky to be bold in your work life, start small. Express some audacity in your personal life—try riding a horse, ordering octopus at a restaurant, joining Toastmasters, snowboarding down a hill, or singing in public. Then take that same energy and channel it to create an audacious business goal for yourself—getting an MBA, creating a new product, making a career change, or buying a company. Allow yourself to consider that this goal *is* possible. If it doesn't create some butterflies in your gut, you're not thinking big enough. And remember: Don't worry about what people think—you're now being shameless! And don't let perceived risks paralyze you, because you're now being brazen!

It can be challenging for overly nice guys to be "tough," but sometimes tough is exactly what's needed. Sometimes being affable and polite just isn't going to get it done. Executive coach Maggie Craddock agrees. "I work with a lot of genuinely nice guys who need some assistance in incredibly competitive corporate environments. I like to remind them of the importance of knowing how to flash a little fang when they need to the most. Not all the time, and not in an inconsiderate display of impulsivity. You need to be strategic about when and how you do it. But there are times when you have to growl, be firm, and push back."

To be bold, overly nice guys must commit to climbing out of the box that's limiting them. It isn't always easy, given how overly nice guys are quick to put the needs (and dreams) of others before their own. Do it differently this time. As Gandhi said, "Be the change you wish to see in the world." Place a high value on your goals and priorities. Passionately pursue your dreams with confidence, courage, and conviction. And, most of all, give yourself permission to shine.

Have you ever interacted with someone who was completely comfortable with being bold and taking risks and been blown away by their audacity? Rob, a lighting contractor, crossed paths with just such an individual in the story below.

### The Rollup

Rob owns a small regional business designing and installing energy-efficient lighting systems for large companies. His friend Calvin, who owns a similar business in a different region, asked him if they could meet and talk about ways to potentially leverage each other for future business. During this discussion, Calvin mentioned that Wayne, his father, was working with him to expand and refine their business plan. Calvin wondered if Rob would be open to talking with his father. *Sure, why not?* thought Rob.

He found Wayne to be a calm, eloquent, confident man. As they talked about the future of the electric-efficiency industry, Wayne commented, "We aren't just changing lights . . . we're changing the world!" Rob was both mesmerized and energized by this man. Not only was Wayne engaging and enthusiastic, but he was also thinking on a whole different level and scale. He was able to conceive of bold new ideas and opportunities for the future that Rob had never considered.

Wayne then took it a step further. He told Rob that he wanted to host a "summit" of various companies in the energy conservation business where direct dialogue and roundtable discussions could take place . . . and Rob was invited to be one of the keynote speakers! This was bending Rob's mind. While Wayne impressed him, he was also baffled, and his head was filled with many questions, such as: *Why* have this summit? *What* in the heck would everyone talk about? And *how* would he get all of these direct and indirect competitors (*paranoid* competitors, at that) together in one room?

Not only did Wayne pull it off, but another result of the summit was a new idea for a cooperative business model instead of a competitive one. Wayne acted as "ringleader" during the summit, deftly using his charisma and intellect to get people to talk and share information in ways that Rob had never dreamed of.

But Wayne's bold vision and actions did not stop there. He used the knowledge and wisdom that he'd gained over many months of information gathering to formulate the idea for a totally new type of "super" energy-service company that would provide a total energy solution—from procurement to delivery to maintenance. He rolled out the idea at a second summit and eventually raised the venture capital to make it happen.

Wayne saw possibilities beyond the obvious. He was willing to think outside the box, be bold, and take educated risks because he knew how to acquire the knowledge he needed to make informed decisions. He was also willing to do the legwork necessary to help those possibilities grow and mature into viable plans. For Wayne, knowledge and ideas were capital, but boldness was the fuel. And his process was essentially repeatable—allowing him to create one successful business venture after another throughout his career.

As the poet Maya Angelou said, "I believe the most important single thing, beyond discipline and creativity, is daring to dare." Wayne was daring in many ways—from brazenly reaching out and talking to numerous experts to bringing these disparate parties together at a summit, and ultimately to turning it into a new business venture and gathering VC support on its behalf. His audacity paid off in a big way.

## NICE GUY STRATEGY: Evangelize

If audacity is the spark that starts the fire, then passion and commitment are the fuel that keeps the fire going. And to generate and sustain a commitment to a big, bold endeavor that goes beyond what is achievable as an individual, it will be necessary to enlist the help of others. You must turn *me* into *we*.

For many overly nice guys, telling more and more people about a bold idea is an audacious act that requires a high level of courage. It's one thing to develop a bold idea in your cubicle or office, but it's quite another to put it "out there" for others to see and judge. Not only are you putting it out there, but you're also asking others to get on board and *participate* with their time, talent, and resources. And the stakes are raised even higher when telling your ideas to people in positions of power, such as corporate executives, investment bankers, the media, or venture capitalists.

To be effective at this type of communication requires skill and savvy. It requires a special kind of speaking up. It requires the ability to evangelize.

To evangelize effectively, you must passionately believe in your project, activity, program, cause, or organization, and then have the ability to articulate its importance and benefits in a compelling way. Others need to buy into your vision enthusiastically and understand why it's in their best interest to get involved. You must have the temerity to get on your soapbox, ask for their help, and get them excited about the audacity of the task at hand.

In the early eighties, Steve Jobs looked to expand Apple Computer from a small start-up company to a major player in the computer industry. As he talked to potential investors and tried to lure experienced executives to the company, he was known to challenge them by asking, "Do you want a chance to change the world?" And then, as he launched the Macintosh (beginning with the infamous "1984" Super Bowl commercial), the charismatic Jobs created a historic buzz by evangelizing—to employees, shareholders, and, most of all, consumers—with a message that said, "This computer is changing the world. Join us." And it did. And they did.

It all starts with the ability to connect and communicate with others. It's a relationship thing, as Alan explains below.

### It's a Relationship Thing

When Alan began his new job as vice president of development at a small West Coast college, he was given the daunting task of increasing gift support at a school where fund-raising had been anemic.

He immediately set the radical goal of doubling the fund to at least $3.5 million in three years. This seemed crazy not only to his staff—which had struggled mightily to raise $1.7 million the previous year—but also to his boss (the college president), who was a little dubious and frustrated with the alumni. He didn't think they had the desire or the wherewithal to support such a lofty goal.

Because of his past success, Alan was confident in his skills and methods. The big "X factor," however, was the people. "One of my guiding principles," he said, "is an old saying that I have pinned to my bulletin board: 'As you lead from the front, don't forget to bring the people with you.' " His most important task was to find the right mix of talent, convince them to set aside their cynicism, build support, and get everyone to buy into his bold vision. "As Jim Collins, author of the best-selling book *Good to Great,* says, 'You've *got* to have the right people on the bus,' " he stressed. "I had to pull together the team that was there, add the right pieces, and give them the right tools.

"And then," he continued, "You need to create an opportunity for enthusiasm, both with the staff and with the donors. You've got to move the donors closer to the institution by evangelizing to them and singing the praises of the school and what we stand for. It's a relationship thing. The more you develop that relationship with donors, the more they become interested in the mission and connected with the institution. And if you're genuine, authentic, and passionate about the school, they pick up on that. It's infectious. They want to be a part of it—and almost always exceed your expectations.

"We more than doubled our endowment in three years," Alan remembered. "Some people say I'm lucky. Well, let me tell you, the more people you contact and the harder you work, the luckier you get."

Alan knew that he had to first set a bold goal and then evangelize—both internally and externally. He needed to get everyone "on the bus" (the bus, metaphorically, was his vision for the growth of the institution) and moving in the same direction. "People will get behind the company if they feel they're really making a difference," says Terry Stinson of Bell Helicopter. As Alan evangelized with his target market—the donors—on behalf of the school, he was able to build a relationship that engaged their participation on behalf of an institution (or mission) they wanted to support.

## NICE GUY STRATEGY: Step-by-Step

Taking on a huge, bold endeavor can be daunting to overly nice guys. Even if they've got an audacious attitude and have enlisted the help of others, they can still feel like they've bitten off *way* more than they can chew. And then, when these feelings of being overwhelmed are added to preexisting insecurity and fear, they just might give up and walk away from a potentially worthwhile endeavor.

A bold action need not require one massive, overwhelming effort. "Little strokes fell great oaks," counseled Benjamin Franklin. With a little planning, the nice guy can break down the project into small, manageable pieces and take small, incremental steps toward a desired outcome.

Breaking down the project into small, discrete pieces helps nice guys bypass the fear that's often associated with big things. It effectively helps you to make meaningful progress toward your goals every day and makes it easier to use your time and energy effectively. This approach also helps with productively managing the time and energy of the team that you've assembled. Ideally, everyone is working in concert, together—step-by-step.

To be effective, sometimes it is necessary to define the tiny pushes that are required from each worker. Deirdre learned that if she wanted her big, bold strategies to be embraced by clients, she first had to break them down into much smaller pieces, as she explained in the following story.

### Taking Smaller Bites

As the president of a major direct marketing firm, Deirdre learned that the high-level strategic plans that she loved to create could sometimes be difficult for clients to absorb. "They'd get overwhelmed," she said. "With one client, whenever I started talking about strategy it seemed like 90 percent of the eyes in the room glazed over. However, once I started talking about smaller, sexier projects like brochures, ad campaigns, and other marketing programs, they perked up and got excited."

For Deirdre, it finally sunk in that people are much better able to digest information when it's spoon-fed in smaller portions. "I've learned to keep the big ideas and big strategies in my head, and then give it to them as small, tactical steps that they can absorb and manage."

Deirdre knows that those small steps are leading to the bigger goal. Meanwhile, the client gets excited about the small "wins" that happen as each project is accomplished. "People need different amounts of information," she said. "I've learned to think strategically but sell tactically in small pieces. It's *much* more effective."

Create a big vision, but make the execution more manageable by breaking it down into small, bite-sized chunks that are easier for you (and others) to grasp and complete. This also gives you the chance to stop and evaluate along the way as milestones are reached and deliverables are met.

As you (and your team) make progress, don't lose focus. Many projects and initiatives can easily distract overly nice guys, but once a priority has been established, encourage them to focus like a laser on achieving the goal. Dare to be a little selfish and give the project the attention and energy it needs. It's similar to the challenge faced by professional athletes as they strive to consistently find the tunnel vision they need to succeed at a high level. Nice guy Cal Ripken shares his thoughts: "In baseball, you wish that you could block out everything else in your life and just concentrate on the field. But life is not that way. There are distractions and there are things that will take away your focus. The key to your success is to be able to balance your life in such a way where you can continue to be motivated and continue to focus at the right time."

### NICE GUY WHIPLASH: Be Bold

Is it possible to think *too* big and be *too* bold? Nice Guy Whiplash can rear its ugly head in several ways, including:

1. *A Hasty Waste.* Moving too fast and with extreme haste can lead to rash decisions that are premature and thoughtless. Being bold is good. Being impetuous and careless is not.

2. *Random Acts of Hubris.* Sometimes ego gets in the way. A lack of humility and perspective can lead to hubris, especially from narcissistic people who tend to lack consideration for others. Overconfidence can lead to laziness, complacency, and not doing your best.

3. *Reckless Wrecks.* A lack of scale, subtlety, appropriateness, and discretion can lead to reckless behavior that can be very damaging to a group and a company. Little or no thought is given to potential ramifications or to the effect that extreme actions might have upon others.

## NICE COMPANY STRATEGIES
# Dive Deeper, Dive Smarter

Take a person who is five feet tall and watch what happens if they're tossed into water that is five feet deep. They'll likely figure out how to get air—be it through swimming or pushing off the bottom and propelling themselves upward. For those who seek a bolder challenge, place them in ten feet of water and see how they fare. For the truly bold and confident, almost any depth becomes manageable and achievable.

Apply this metaphor to the business world. Before tossing employees into deep water, smart organizations provide necessary tools and skills—such as swimming lessons, diving gear, inflatable life rafts, and shark repellent. The point is to systematically inspire people to take chances and grow within an environment that demonstrates its commitment to development and risk taking. For overly nice guys, encouraging them in this way will significantly influence their ability to reach their true potential. It will allow them to see the world from a new perspective and make different choices.

Some business leaders take a binary view of this issue—people are bold or they are not. Others employ strategies that systematically promote boldness and encourage their employees—including overly nice guys—to ease into deeper waters without fear of drowning. These wise leaders recognize that while minor losses may be experienced in the short run, in the long run they're setting a precedent for innovation, change, and

> **JON LUTHER, CEO, DUNKIN' BRANDS**
>
> Nice guys . . . must pick a couple of spots that extend beyond their comfort zone—and then get used to it.

growth. Despite some of the occasional discomfort that might be experienced, when overly nice guys are achieving more success by virtue of their bold new ways, there is a high likelihood that their organization will benefit as well.

Jon Luther of Dunkin' Brands states, "Nice guys must stretch outside of their comfort zones. They must pick a couple of spots that extend beyond their comfort zone—and then get used to it. With small and manageable bold steps, their behavior ultimately begins to change." Luther stresses the importance of the company providing support for those bold steps. The level of support will be determined by the nature of the organization coupled with its tolerance for diving deeper. For example, a pharmaceutical company such as Pfizer must continually push its scientists to be as bold as possible when exploring new drug programs. However, the packaging and safety of the products must be highly controlled due the regulatory nature of the industry. In comparison, a new genre of Web search-engine companies may aggressively provide an environment where *everyone* embraces bold new ideas.

### NICE COMPANY STRATEGY: Create a Dive Plan

Ask most CEOs if they would like their employees to be bolder and to dive *deeper* than ever before, and they will likely answer, "Yes."

Ask most CEOs if they have ever created or implemented programs that push their employees to be bolder and to dive smarter than in the past, and they will likely answer, "Huh? What do you mean?" Or, "It's ingrained in our culture."

If your organization has a program that systematically pushes people—including overly nice guys—to be bolder, you are in rare company. Today, most boldness "programs" consist of an informal executive management philosophy. When the substance of a program is simply represented by a philosophy, it's lacking a systematic process that can be reproduced, managed, and measured effectively. In the absence of such a process, employees will typically fall back on old default behaviors that inhibit overly nice guys from diving into deeper waters.

On the other hand, if you introduce programs that complement your organization's (presumed) philosophy of boldness, you will get very different results. As you create a Dive Plan for overly nice guys, you are instituting a systematic program that inspires overly nice guys to be bolder, dive deeper, and dive smarter.

Dive Plans can be managed and measured. When creating one, a number of variables can impact its design. For overly nice guys, we typically recommend that the following three factors be considered:

1. *Provide a Platform.* With a supportive culture in place, your organization can *systematically* promote the importance of being bold. Through incentive programs (financial, vacation time, etc.), recognition (awards, publicity, etc.), and other outreach strategies, let people know that they have the opportunity to dive deeper and be bolder, and are strongly encouraged to do so.

2. *Group Dives.* Overly nice guys have a tendency to shy away from the spotlight. To counter this tendency, it may be appropriate to push and demonstrate bold behavior via groups (as compared to just the individuals). Since there is often comfort in numbers, people are more likely to step up and feel persuaded to take on a bold new challenge if they are part of a team. Joe McGuire of Tweeter is a big proponent of this approach. "You have to learn to accomplish your objectives through others. And there's no faster way to rally a team of people to accomplish an almost impossible task than to define the task, talk about the benefit, and then talk about the fact that the whole world thinks this

can't be done. Tell them, 'It's impossible, but we're going to go do it!' " There's a reason why people dive in groups: it provides additional safety and motivation. You are able to leverage the knowledge of others, and in the face of fear you have others to count on.

3. *Every Dive Matters.* Every time an overly nice guy dives deeper, it is very helpful to review the outcome of his or her effort—even if it was negative. This can be an evaluation-oriented activity such as a formal debriefing process after a bold step has been taken, or it can be an informal discussion or comment. The point is to *consistently* recognize the effort and to provide feedback. At Southwest Airlines, a program has been implemented that mandates that any recommendation made by *any* employee receive an immediate and thoughtful response. Herb Kelleher notes, "Every idea—no matter how far-fetched, how wild, or how out of the ballpark—has to be responded to promptly and respectfully. And the reason for that is that they'll never get any more ideas if you don't encourage that." When you stop responding, people eventually stop trying.

## NICE COMPANY STRATEGY: Deepwater Diving

Metaphorically speaking, when it comes to diving into the "water," overly nice guys will have definite depth preferences. In some cases, they will prefer to stay on land. In other cases, they will choose to go deeper than ever before. In a large part, their desire to dive will be significantly influenced through the support that you provide in your organization.

If the tolerance level is low when it comes to taking risks and diving deeper, people will limit themselves to shallower water. If you encourage them to take bold risks and explore unlimited depths, a few people may flounder or even drown, but many more will thrive in significant ways. The payoff can be huge. Your organization must find an approach that reflects an acceptable tolerance level for the company and inspires overly nice guys within it to get bolder and more effective.

Organizationally, there are a number of steps that help overly nice guys dive deeper. These steps are dependent upon your organization's tolerance levels.

1. *Depth Levels.* Define specific depth levels that denote where people align in their desire to take bold steps. As a starting point, we have identified four depth levels: (1) landlocked, (2) shallow divers, (3) deep divers, and (4) open-water divers. As the employee gains comfort and confidence with one level, he or she can be encouraged to dive more deeply.

2. *Lifeboat Strategies.* If you are going to teach people to dive deeper, provide a recovery mechanism in case something goes wrong. If you have a shallow diver who is flailing in open waters, make sure you employ a lifeboat strategy that brings him back to the appropriate depth level and prepares him for going deeper only when appropriate. For overly nice guys, identify a strategy that motivates them to learn from their previous dive and try again. For your business (or customer or supplier), be prepared to counteract the impact of people who dove too deeply (and to perform damage control on the decisions they made).

While deeper dives are interesting, it is even more interesting to see your nice guys and your organization excel as a result of becoming bolder. Regardless of whether "depth levels" work or don't work for your company, put systems in place that incite overly nice guys to go bigger, go bolder, and go deeper.

## Chapter Summary

### NICE GUY MOTIVES AND SYMPTOMS

**Fear of Failure**  Overly nice guys often do not want to take big bold steps because they become overly fixated on their fear of failure or potential failure.

**Comfort Zone Paralysis**  Overly nice guys are loath to extend themselves beyond their comfort zones and, as a result, don't reap the rewards from taking some bolder steps.

**Attention Avoidance**  Many overly nice guys don't want attention drawn to themselves, so they would prefer to see others get rewarded.

### NICE GUY STRATEGIES

**Audacity**  Overly nice guys must develop the ability to be audacious at times when they want to take bold steps. They will need to summon the courage to push beyond their comfort zones when the time is right.

**Evangelize**  Overly nice guys must, either individually or through the assistance of others, evangelize their bold ideas. They need to get people excited by the prospect of their offerings and spread the word accordingly.

**Step-by-Step**  Audacity and evangelism as well as other boldness techniques don't require everything to be done at once. Bold steps can be taken through the accumulation of smaller, more controlled steps.

### NICE COMPANY STRATEGIES

**Creating a**
**Dive Plan**

Organizationally, you must create the mind-set, processes, and environment to entice people to take bold actions. If these are not in place, overly nice guys in your company will be much less likely to take a deep dive into new and bold areas.

**Deepwater**
**Diving**

As you help your nice guys take bolder steps and achieve more success, it is important that you don't push them well beyond their capacity. Specifically, work with them to identify how deep they are willing to dive and manage to that accordingly.

YOU HAVE THE RIGHT TO:

# Win

[
COMPETE AND
SUCCEED
]

## NICE GUY SYNDROME

# To Get the Corner Office, Nice Guys Need to Learn How to Win

Overly nice guys often aren't comfortable with the concept of "winning," so they resist it. When placed squarely in a competitive situation, they feel guilty that a "winner" and "loser" will be part of the outcome. Whether because of competitive pressure, a sense of unworthiness, a fear of sowing the seeds of future conflict, or concern over displacing others, many overly nice guys will shun the limelight and the winner's circle.

Choosing to win (or lose) can have ramifications for the overly nice guy and everyone else involved. When trying to be nice, it can be difficult to accept winning while others lose. Overly nice guys want to see others succeed—which is noble—but when it's at the expense of their own deserved success (and their company's success), it usually doesn't serve the greater good.

This is not to say that overly nice guys are inherently "losers." They are often extremely intelligent and talented people who experience success and win. But they can win more often and in bigger ways without compromising their ethics, self-respect, and integrity.

## The Stories

The following two stories, inspired by actual events, illustrate a few of the "win" challenges that nice guys face in the business world. What would *you* do? Would you be able to win graciously and fairly in these situations? How might you go about winning in a constructive way? Would you be able to commit to more wins in the future?

### Promoting the Promotion of Another

Randall was a very talented executive. During his ten years with the firm, he had contributed a great deal of value in terms of accomplished work and innovation. When a position opened up for a new team leader, Randall seemed like a very good choice, at least to everyone except perhaps himself. "You should really consider that position, Randall," Joyce, a colleague, was saying. "You've earned it! You'd be *perfect* for the job—given your background and experience." Randall felt a little embarrassed by Joyce's encouraging words and he realized that there were other managers who would be seeking the position. He also wondered if he really would be the most deserving candidate should he apply.

Nevertheless, after several other colleagues related the same kind of encouragement, Randall decided to throw his hat in the ring for the position. A few weeks later he learned that he was one of two final candidates who were being seriously considered. He was invited to meet Sharon, the senior executive to whom the new venture team leader would report. He also learned that Greg was the other finalist. When he entered Sharon's office for the interview, Randall couldn't help thinking about Greg's long tenure with the firm and his strong performance record. He respected Greg and believed that he deserved the kind of opportunity that the new position would provide.

After Sharon reviewed the basic responsibilities and her expectations for the team leader position, she focused in on Randall's qualifications for the job. She was very complimentary about his past contributions and made it clear that she thought that Randall could be very effective in the role. At the same time, she said that she thought Greg was a very strong candidate as well. Then she surprised Randall by asking if he would be willing to recommend Greg for the position and to write a letter in support of his candidacy. Randall didn't know at the time that Sharon was asking Greg to do the same thing for Randall. She explained, given Randall's ten years in the firm and knowledge of the contributions of various managers such as Greg, that his assessment would be very helpful.

Ultimately, Randall not only gave a strong recommendation for Greg during the interview but also wrote a very strong letter in support of him for the promotion. In fact, as Randall wrote the recommendation letter, he couldn't help feeling not only that Greg deserved the promotion but that he would personally feel bad if he cost Greg the job by getting the promotion himself. While Randall knew the team leader position would be a strong positive step in his own career, he felt very uncomfortable with the idea that winning the role would mean Greg would have to lose it. Little did Randall know that Greg declined to write a letter on his behalf. Greg wanted the job and knew that career advancement sometimes meant competition and winners and losers.

In the end, based in part on Randall's strong recommendation, Greg got the promotion. This was disappointing to many people in the organization, the majority of whom (especially the members on the team he would have led) believed Randall was more qualified and would have made a better team leader.

## Backing Down and Going Backward

Elena had always had a difficult time with disagreements. She disliked winning an argument if it meant she caused someone else to feel bad. In one notable case, she was appointed to research and then recommend a new service plan for the chain of electronic stores for which she worked. Consistent with her usual conscientious, thorough style, she talked to many salespeople and other employees from across the firm as she developed a new plan that she thought would be optimal. She also carefully studied the old service plan and reviewed both the financial history and the customer feedback connected with it. Eventually she developed a streamlined and relatively simple plan that seemed to capture the strengths of what had been previously used. It also eliminated some complicated details that many customers had complained about.

In the end, she made a recommendation for a service plan that she believed could be competitively priced and provide the kind of reassurance and support that would be attractive to customers. When she presented this to upper management, she was surprised at the response. In particular, Ross (a vice president) was very vocal and critical. "I don't like it," he said. "I don't think we could price it high enough, and our service agreements have been one of our highest margin and most profitable product categories," he argued. "Besides, I think it's too easy to understand. Like it or not, excessive details and a bit of ambiguity create the kind of anxious motivation that customers sometimes need to be willing to pay the extra money to sign up for a service plan just in case they have a problem."

"Yes, I understand you are resistant to the kind of changes I am proposing," Elena countered, "but the sales of our existing service plan have been steadily declining. And we have a number of customer complaints that suggest that once they leave the store and have a chance to read and think about it more closely, they feel it is a poor value. Wouldn't a more affordable plan—one that is easy to understand and that provides more value—increase our sales and promote customer loyalty at the same time? I could envision some customers choosing our electronics over our competitors' partly because they know they would have more peace of mind when buying expensive items like a high-definition TV or a new stereo system."

At this point, while the nonverbal behavior of the group generally seemed responsive to her arguments, Ross looked more displeased than ever. Now his ego was on the line. "We live and die by margins, I tell you. This proposal is not in our best interest if we want to make a solid profit on these plans. Besides, didn't the sales on our service agreements actually go up last month? I think we should work with what we already have in place and maybe add a couple of new twists, especially if we can ratchet the price up a few more bucks!" he said with conviction.

Elena knew that the reason sales went up the previous month was primarily because of a major storewide sale the chain had run and due to a special promotion on the service plan in particular. But she said nothing. She felt uncomfortable trying to argue her point of view when it was obvious that Ross was now feeling defensive. Despite all the work she had put into developing a new service plan that she was convinced could be great for their customers, she didn't want to win the debate if it meant she had to "beat" Ross. She wasn't up for a fight.

In the end, the group decided to keep the old plan in place. Some members of the management group were nearly convinced to support Elena's proposal, but when she did not follow up on her position during the meeting, they concluded that she must have been persuaded to Ross's point of view. Consequently, a year later, sales on service plans continued their decline, and customer complaints were further on the rise. In addition, sales of electronics were down as well. And Elena had not been offered any other opportunities to head up new efforts for the company.

## The Motives and Symptoms

Randall and Elena both appear to have good reasons for being uncomfortable with winning. They are "nice" people in general and don't like the idea of causing someone else to experience the unpleasant feelings of being a "loser." Randall was very interested in being promoted to the new venture team leadership position, but he was even more concerned that he not cost Greg the job. Even though most people close to the situation felt that Randall was better qualified, it was Randall's advocating of Greg—in the spirit of being a supportive and nice person—that seemed to make the difference.

Elena had worked hard to come up with a new service plan that could help her company and its customers, but she was too uncomfortable about winning her disagreement with Ross. When winning means others have to lose, nice people like Elena often become self-sacrificing by simply not standing up for themselves and their point of view.

Unfortunately, nice guys' reluctance to win can be costly. There are times when they need their viewpoints to be heard and to win the day for the good of most people connected to the situation. Randall could have done much good had he been promoted to team leader, but this meant he had to win the competition with Greg. His reluctance to put forth the necessary effort to win not only cost Randall the promotion, it also cost his potential team members the leader they seemed to want.

Meanwhile, Elena's new service plan seemed to be just what her firm and its customers needed to resolve the problems with the old plan. Her decision not to stand up to Ross and help her well-researched proposal win the day made her company—and its employees—all losers in the end. The resistance that nice people have to winning is a particularly challenging part of the Nice Guy Syndrome. Why? Because it represents a culmination of many of the other syndrome challenges discussed throughout this book.

There are several symptoms related to nice guy tendencies to avoid winning that involve various behaviors and emotions. Here we will highlight three key symptoms.

1. *Deference to Others.* Since overly nice people are uncomfortable with standing up for their viewpoint when confronted by others with different opinions, they tend to defer to the people competing with them. They allow others' needs to take priority over their own. Overly nice guys seem to view themselves as unworthy and other people as more valuable. And they often simply shut down when coworkers assert a position in opposition to their own, even when the overly nice guys are more experienced and better qualified. As a result, this tendency of overly nice guys to defer to the will of others can end up creating problems for everyone in their organization who depends upon their input.

2. *Reluctance to Create Losers.* Overly nice people don't like to cause others to lose, even if they themselves win. Instead of looking out for their own self-interest, they tend to be excessively concerned with not offending others or hurting their feelings. As a result, instead of aggressively seeking the "winning" solution that is best for the business, they often choose the least offensive course of action. Unfortunately, this can make losers of everyone connected to the situation.

3. *Diminishing Oneself.* Nice guys act from the seemingly noble intention of being nice to others, even those who are in competition with them. Unfortunately, this "nice" stance diminishes them and the contributions they could be making to their organizations (and their colleagues). This is perhaps the most fundamentally troubling symptom of being overly nice. Genuinely nice people who have real value to bring to their organizations—as well as to their customers and clients—negate that value when they diminish themselves. Yet, it is the very act of diminishing themselves that is at the heart of the Nice Guy Syndrome.

Both Randall and Elena avoided winning in what they seemed to think was the spirit of being "nice." It's a natural tendency for overly nice people to avoid winning. But these two cases illustrate the flaw in this stance. Sometimes a viewpoint or position needs to win out in order to serve the greater good for all involved. Successful business requires that decisions be made, even when it means that some viewpoints will not be selected. And nice guys will have the best point of view for given circumstances at least some of the time. This means that they need to learn to win. Win graciously and fairly, yes, but win nevertheless. In the following section, we offer several nice guy strategies that can help them to learn to win.

## NICE GUY STRATEGIES
## Give Yourself Permission to Win

Business rewards those who have the right angle, the right commitment, and the right skills to drive success—and win. To be *effectively* nice, overly nice guys must learn to understand, accept, and embrace winning. They must learn to assert themselves, little by little, and gradually gain the ability to win in bigger and bigger ways. The world is not served when capable people diminish their own talents and intelligence. Overly nice guys owe it to themselves (and to others) to do their best at all times and embrace winning.

Overly nice guys need to aim higher, risk "failure," and learn that it is acceptable, honorable, and desirable for them to be on the winning side of the equation. While a win-win situation is ideal, overly nice guys should take pride in doing their best and winning even when someone else loses. They can develop a comfort level that allows them to recognize and enjoy the virtues of winning. And as overly nice guys apply the principles of excellence, decency, and fairness in their work and embrace quality results, they encourage others to do better by setting the bar higher.

## NICE GUY STRATEGY: Failure

Would you rather be a failure or a success? Ridiculous question? "Of course everyone wants to be a success and no one wants to be a failure," you may respond. But wait. Actually, the two are much closer to each other than you might think. In fact, if you want to achieve meaningful success—success in which you learn, grow, and make significant contributions; where your life is full, counts for something, and makes a difference—you will have to fail sometimes. There are no exceptions to this rule.

*Significant success requires failure*, but failure from a whole new perspective. According to Jim Tressel, head football coach at Ohio State University, "Every time you're tested and every time you're bruised and battered, it's always good for you. In life or in football, you learn more in your suffering than you do in your wonderful moments." This is difficult to grasp for overly nice guys, whose natural fear of failure is a symptom of Nice Guy Syndrome—a symptom that holds them back from being bold and taking risks.

Most people—including overly nice guys—dread the idea of being labeled a "failure." Because they have an excessive concern with how others perceive them and don't want to disappoint people who are counting on them, the risk of failure can paralyze nice guys and cause them to quit. In the words of Eleanor Roosevelt, "No one can make you feel inferior without your consent." Unfortunately, overly nice guys *give* their consent and allow failure to let them feel inferior and defeated.

It is only through risking failure, however, that most of life's greatest successes are achieved. Seeming failures can be a powerful way to learn and are almost always a fruitful stepping-stone to life's greatest breakthroughs and successes. They are an essential part of life and are usually just *challenges in progress*. And when overly nice guys learn this important lesson, they come to understand that the only *real* failure is when they back away from worthwhile challenges without giving their best effort. In fact, one of the *nicest* things they can do to benefit themselves and their colleagues is to choose to take risks wisely—with failure as a possible outcome—in the pursuit of meaningful and lasting achievement.

"Once you have determined that people have the basic intelligence and the basic drive to succeed, then what you have to do is give them a chance to fail," says Terry Stinson of Bell Helicopter. "Most of the time, they will not. And if they do . . . that's fine. You learn. You move on. But you cannot get in their way."

The following story illustrates these ideas. As a project team member, Elston needed to step up to the plate and risk failure. His team needed him.

### Opportunity Knocks

Elston was a key member of a three-person team that had worked for several months on a new corporate knowledge management system. Finally, the day arrived for proposing the system to the top management team. If given the green light, the new system would be installed and used by a large division of the company.

The plan was for Stephen, the project leader, to make the presentation. Elston and Marie, the other project members, were present for support and to help answer questions. While Stephen clearly had the best overall sense of the project and the strongest presentation skills to help assure a successful presentation, Elston had done much of the research and prepared most of the documentation to support their proposal. In fact, Elston arguably was the most technically informed team member.

Unfortunately, shortly before the presentation, Elston and Marie were informed that Stephen had a family emergency and might not make it in time for the meeting. When they entered the conference room, they glanced at each other nervously and looked in all directions for any sign of Stephen. At last, the senior manager called the meeting to order. After noting Stephen's emergency and the difficulty he realized this posed for the team in presenting their proposal, he explained that the presentation needed to proceed nonetheless to avoid delays. He then turned it over to Elston and Marie. They stared at each other for several tense moments, each hoping the other would step forward to make the presentation. While Elston realized he was the better informed of the two, he was temporarily paralyzed by the idea of making a presentation for which he was not prepared. The thought of failure and rejection froze him in his seat.

Gradually, however, he summoned his courage. He realized that he was, in fact, the team's best chance to meet the challenge and that he needed to step forward and risk failure. He took a deep breath, nodded to Marie to indicate he would take the floor, and walked to the front of the room. *The key is that I do the best that I can,* he thought to himself.

He started off feeling pretty shaky as he provided an overview of the proposal, but eventually he hit his stride. The meeting settled into a productive conversation as attendees peppered him with questions about the key points. Elston gradually gained confidence and responded more effectively to each new question.

In the end, his presentation won the day. The management team was impressed with Elston's knowledge of the subject and even complimented him on filling in to make the presentation in Stephen's absence. Eventually, the proposal was approved with only slight modifications. And Elston's risk of failure by making the presentation on such short notice marked a turning point in his career. Not only did he gain confidence for meeting future unexpected challenges, but he had caught the eye of management and set the stage for a big promotion a few months later.

Risking failure and learning from small setbacks along the way are key parts of learning to win. Overly nice guys need to face the reality that rejection and setbacks are unavoidable parts of everyday life. We all fail. And not just a little, but a lot, especially when taking risks and learning new skills that enable us to meet exciting and worthwhile challenges. Overly nice guys have to get tougher and be willing to plunge ahead in spite of the bumps in the road. George Naddaff of Boston Market wonders, "How many people fail because they hate rejection? You have got to harden yourself. And the way you get hardened is getting over

the word *no*." Understanding that difficult times can offer significant opportunities for success is an important part of gaining
wisdom.

Soichiro Honda, the founder of the Honda Motor Company,
gained this kind of wisdom in his own life. After growing up
in poverty and seeing several of his siblings die of starvation,
Honda encountered several other dramatic setbacks. His original
piston plant was bombed in 1945. Later, it was completely de-
stroyed during an earthquake. His personal philosophy of success
evolved from these catastrophic events. Because of his life and
career setbacks, he learned to embrace and be transformed by failure. In a speech he made when receiving an honorary doctorate at
the University of Michigan, he stated, "Many people dream of
success. To me, success can only be achieved through repeated failure and introspection. In fact, success represents the one percent
of your work that results from the ninety-nine percent that is
called failure."*

We all fail, especially if we take risks, try to develop new skills,
and take on exciting and worthwhile challenges. How can we get
beyond the failure without letting it get us down and paralyze us?
By learning how to develop a selective memory. Glean all the lessons you can from defeat, then forget it—but keep the lesson.
Move on and focus on the next challenge.

In baseball, when the relief pitcher blows the lead in the ninth
inning and loses the game, the next day he must have selective
memory and forget his failure from the night before. If he does, he
can then take the field during his next game with the confidence
and resolve he needs to be successful. "The test of success is not
what you do when you're on top," said General George S. Patton Jr.

---

\* This example is included on the audio program *Unlimited Energy* by Peter
McLaughlin (Niles, IL: Nightengale-Conant Corporation, 1998).

"Success is how high you bounce when you hit bottom. You're never beaten until you admit it."

## NICE GUY STRATEGY: Excellence

For a moment, let's shift our mind-set away from "winning" and "losing" and instead consider "better" and "best." Yes, it's gratifying to land the deal, get the promotion, or win the game. But regardless of whether you won or lost, did you do your absolute best work?

The Greek derivation of the word *compete* is "to fly with." Competition is a good thing. The greater good is served when quality is encouraged and people excel at a high level. The best ideas deserve to "win." The top solutions benefit your company and benefit the world, so encourage the cream to rise to the top within the organization. Support the best idea regardless of ownership. "It's not about *who* is right, it's about *what* is right," says Dan Gilbert, owner of the Cleveland Cavaliers and CEO of Quicken Loans.

Fight for your ideas if you believe in them. It's not about ego; it's about good business. Given the tendency of overly nice guys to limit themselves and defer to others, this is often easier said than done. Ultimately, doing your best is an *inside* job, not an *outside* competition. No one is served when overly nice guys diminish themselves and play small—not your team, not your organization, and not the world. Instead, play big. Think of winning as a competition between your current performance and your highest potential or personal best. Strive for excellence and create a mind-set where you always give your top effort and do your finest work. Give yourself permission to win . . . and know that you are worthy of that win.

It's important for nice guys to know and believe that they can compete *and* win without sacrificing their dignity or integrity. "Business—whether we like it or not—includes competition," says Sam DiPiazza of PricewaterhouseCoopers. "It is challenging, aggressive, and very demanding. And despite the perception of many, it can also be performed nicely. Everyone has a choice as to how they conduct business. If remaining nice is a goal, it can be achieved respectfully and successfully. The bottom line is that you don't have to be an SOB to successfully compete."

Finding that balance between competition and civility can be tricky, as Michael relates in the following story.

### An Inside Job

As executive director of the American Heart Association of Vermont, Michael was often in situations where he seemingly "competed" for money against other nonprofits in the state. "Sometimes I'd hear people say, 'Why did they give to cancer and not to us?' I hate that mind-set—that there's a limited amount of money that we all vie for. I hate limited thinking like that. If *we* do things right, the money will come."

For himself and his organization, Michael encourages a mind-set with an internal focus. "It's about *us,* not about *them,*" he said. "What do *we* have to do? What are the conversations *we* have to have to lock up the community and get people to support us?" The job, as Michael sees it, is to focus on goals, process, and behavior—"the DNA of our organization," he calls it. It's an internal focus on *What can we do better?* "I know that there's sufficient money out there," he said, "but internally are we lined up as we need to be to go after it? Are we lined up to excel and give our very best effort? Winning is an inside job, not an outside one."

This frame of mind can be difficult to instill within an organization if everyone is already immersed in the mind-set that "there isn't enough" and "resources are limited." One organization's "win" seems to come at the expense of another. However, as Michael sees it, if a potential donor is so moved, they could decide to give to *both* the American Cancer Society and the American Heart Association, could they not? So the key is to encourage excellence, do your absolute best as an organization, and believe that the money will follow.

Embracing a mind-set that values excellence and hard work can be transformative for overly nice guys—many of whom are extremely intelligent and talented but lack the cutthroat instincts of the SOBs of the world. Know and believe that it's your job—your *mission*, even—to bring the best ideas forward and ensure that they get the visibility they deserve. If this mind-set is spread throughout your organization, it will breed a corporate culture that expects, demands, and rewards excellence. It will also promote the notion of "effectively nice" people. If there is an implicit agreement from the top down that excellence always comes first, then the primary criteria for judging ideas will always be excellence—*not* who talks the loudest or blows the most smoke.

**NICE GUY STRATEGY: Recognition**

Nice guys are good team players and like to share credit and rewards when appropriate. They play nice, they play fair, and they show good sportsmanship. They usually collaborate well and are deft at supporting the common good and seeking out win-win situations.

So, where is the problem?

Overly nice guys tend to have big hearts and small egos. They don't always realize that it's healthy and appropriate to receive credit for one's achievements—and be rewarded for them, too. They rarely self-promote or seek recognition. Instead, they are much more likely to be generous and self-effacing and to give credit to others. It just doesn't occur to an overly nice guy to grab attention or credit—until the ugly moment arises when an aggressive coworker takes credit for his or her work. This hits him hard—like a punch to the gut. *That was my idea!* the nice guy will think. *I did 90 percent of the work, and that jerk didn't even mention my name during the big presentation to the boss!* If this continues, eventually the undeserving coworker might even grab a promotion or pay raise that should have gone to the more deserving nice guy. He or she will feel hurt, angry, and betrayed—like a doormat that others walk on. This leaves the overly nice guy feeling discouraged, depleted, and defeated.

How can the nice guy get the visibility and credit he or she deserves without being taken advantage of by obnoxious brownnosers, big blowhards, sneaky weasels, or arrogant jerks? One of the best ways to avoid this problem is to simply avoid working with brownnosers, blowhards, weasels, and jerks. Deirdre developed this talent earlier in her career, and it has served her well—as she shares in the following story.

### Picking the People

Throughout her career, Deirdre had never been one to seek out recognition, raises, promotions, or new opportunities. As a shy, introverted person, she hated phonies and shameless self-promoters. Yet rewards and opportunities always seemed to find her—thanks to her personal strategy that she calls "picking the people."

"I always seemed to align myself with people who are smart, talented, and considerate," she said. "I chose people who are genuinely committed to top quality and making sure that the best ideas are supported. People like these have high integrity and less ego, and they aren't threatened by other strong, intelligent people. They are also the type of people who give recognition to others. They are always pushing me forward to get more visibility. They recognize how good you are and appreciate you."

Deirdre continued, "I never made a career decision based on money or short-term opportunity. Instead, I picked the people. I'd much rather pick my boss than pick an account to work on. I made the decision to consciously align myself with like-minded people. For instance, I'd be extremely impressed with someone and say to myself, *I'm going to work for that person* . . . and eventually I would! And then I'd gain unbelievable skills by working for them."

Picking the people has added benefits down the road. "Over time, a funny thing happens," added Deirdre. "When these people who you've 'picked' move on, they pick you! They take their people with them. You get recruited by them and chosen for great opportunities. In fact, you don't ever have to apply for jobs if you do it right. Just about all of these people with whom I aligned myself became close friends, and two of them became my longtime business partners. I could not have won bigger."

Deirdre's strategy can be incredibly effective. She consciously chooses with whom she wishes to align herself—and has faith that, in the long run, they will help lead her where she wants to go. In the meantime, she spends her time working with people she respects while focusing on work she loves instead of wasting time and energy with office politics and self-promotion.

But what if you have to work with less-than-noble people who don't seem to have your best interests at heart? Yes, it will be important to speak up, confront, or set a boundary as you must— especially if it's a grievous situation where the stakes are high—but, ultimately, it's much better for the overly nice guy to avoid dysfunctional petty situations from the beginning. Why battle against a weasel over who gets the "credit." You may get a short-term win, but in the long run it's hard to outweasel a weasel. These battles actually energize the weasel but leave the nice guy feeling drained and discouraged.

Getting beyond the issue of credit, it is much more important to consistently face situations with strength, confidence, and dignity. Ultimately, it's about taking ownership of your work, your career, and your life. Instead of feeling disrespected because your manager took credit for your work while making a presentation to the VP, insist upon making the presentation and speaking on your own behalf the next time such an opportunity arises. Be bold and take responsibility for bringing your own ideas forward to upper management. Or, better yet, start your own business and be the boss! Don't wait around for others to recognize you. Find your own voice and claim what's yours.

## NICE GUY WHIPLASH: Win

It's important to keep things in perspective when it comes to winning. Going too far with an obsessive desire to win can have severe consequences. This type of Nice Guy Whiplash takes many forms, including the following:

1. *Scorched Earth.* Fueled by greed, this is a "win at all costs" attitude that lays waste to everything in its path in pursuit of the win—leaving nothing but scorched earth in its wake. This approach leaves one to ask, "At what cost did I achieve this so-called win?"

2. *Ego-Tripping.* Narcissism is the mask that covers a deep insecurity that can be satiated only by winning. Pride, vanity, and a raging ego drive a constant need for attention. Egomaniacs don't

share credit with others and tend to lack appreciation for the efforts of others.

3. *Mean, with Envy.* Resenting the success of others (and coveting it) can leave you feeling bitter and angry. A sense of entitlement can drive people to think that the credit should have been theirs.

4. *Overconfidence.* An excessive amount of cockiness and arrogance leads people to assume that past success will naturally lead to present and future wins. They don't take the competition seriously, which can cause laziness, complacency, and a tendency to not do their best.

5. *Credit Grabbers.* These credit-hungry people grab an undue share of the credit. They often do an excessive amount of self-promotion. An example of this is a boss who takes credit with superiors for the work of subordinates without giving them recognition.

## NICE COMPANY STRATEGIES
# Untapped Potential

As a business executive, you have a responsibility to maximize the success of your business. As a business leader, you have a responsibility to provide your entire team with an opportunity to win. As a business manager, you are failing on both counts if you do not maximize the potential of overly nice guys in your organization.

NGS survey results indicate that 61 percent of respondents feel they are overly nice, while 50 percent believe their bosses are overly nice. Based upon these statistics, a conscious and deliberate effort to help overly nice guys "win" can be one of the greatest services you'll provide for your organization.

So why is it so easy to look the other way? Why don't organizations

spend more time training overly nice guys to push themselves harder
for the big win? Often it's because the nice guys just aren't visible.
Meanwhile, attention is diverted toward those claiming responsibility for the wins—justified or unjustified. For the justified winners,
their contributions should be duly recognized and set as a precedent
for others to follow. For the unjustified, there is a high probability
that one or more overly nice guys are behind the curtain avoiding
the spotlight. As a leader, try to make sure that the right people receive the proper recognition.

Jack Bogle, founder of The Vanguard Group, promotes the notion that "everyone should participate in winning, regardless of
the size of the win." He prefers to emphasize the importance of his
team's collective contributions and stresses that everyone should
take an active role in making a difference.

In some instances, overly nice guys perceive the notion of
"winning" as a negative experience. It might be because they
struggle with the idea that a coworker might lose if they win. Or
perhaps they're turned off by Credit Grabbers who steal the show
and are unjustly rewarded for a win. Either way, a vicious cycle
begins that stifles creativity and inaccurately gives credit to the
wrong people while overly nice guys get lost in the woodwork.
When this happens, the company harbors a group of people whose
potential is untapped and ignored—at a significant disservice to
the organization. But there are ways to address this common
problem.

**NICE COMPANY STRATEGY: Healthy Competition**

Healthy competition can be a positive and motivating influence
within your organization. It inspires people to be their best and to
do so in an ethical fashion. It provides the motivation to work toward a common goal to the benefit of the entire organization. And

healthy competition can (and should) include overly nice guys. It is an important ingredient for business success.

Unhealthy competition, on the other hand, reeks of selfishness and a disregard for the good of the company (in favor of the good for an individual). When choices are made and shortcuts are taken by someone seeking to win purely for the sake of his or her own glory and gain, it's unhealthy competition. It torpedoes company goals, sets a poor (and sometimes dangerous) example, and is demoralizing for those who are team players. It subverts those who are honest and authentic and places them in compromising and defensive positions. Ultimately, the corporate culture is poisoned.

Discerning the differences between healthy and unhealthy competition becomes one of your biggest challenges. When overly nice guys develop an appreciation for healthy competition and embrace it, they will more vigorously pursue winning. It's also crucial that they know that they can pursue winning while also staying true to their values and ethics. When asked about the need for healthy competition, Bert Jacobs, cofounder of *Life is good,* said, "Humility is important to us at *Life is good.* We are competitive people. We work hard and we like to win. However, the only time we look down on someone else is when we're helping them up." For *Life is good,* winning is not just about the dollars, it is also about philanthropic endeavors and spreading "the vibe" around the world in meaningful and ethical ways. *Life is good* sees the need for competition—as long as it is healthy.

When implemented correctly, healthy competition can become an integral part of your organization with the help of the following steps:

1. *The Collective Team Win.* The majority of the professional world is composed of teams that collaborate in different capacities. When someone wins, actively put forth an effort to acknowledge

the entire team. Even if the lead spokesperson is the only person willing to stand up and speak, it is crucial that the team be recognized. Overly nice guys are often more comfortable receiving credit as a team instead of as an individual as they'd rather share the spotlight than be singled out.

2. *Losers Still Win.* Even when healthy competition is embraced, overly nice guys will feel reticent about others "losing" as a result of their win. While a loss is a loss, the losing party can learn a great deal from their failure. The key is to do this in a tactful and growth-oriented way. If you let someone walk away from a loss without exploring possible improvements and without making it a learning experience, you miss a huge opportunity.

3. *Coworker Friendships.* Winning becomes even more difficult for overly nice guys when their "opponents" are their friends. They will often avoid winning in order to avoid hurting their feelings. They are doing a disservice to themselves and their coworkers, however, if the overly nice guy has the best ideas or is best suited for the promotion. Doug Walker of REI believes strongly in this philosophy and even goes as far to say, "You shouldn't let your friendships get in the way of pursuing the best strategy for the company." It is also reasonable to question the authenticity of any relationship if someone feels that it is necessary to hold themselves back in favor of letting their "friend" get ahead.

So, when coaching overly nice guys to better embrace winning, extol the virtues of healthy competition. Let them know that by pushing themselves to excel at a high level and win, they are making their company and the people who work for the company stronger and more successful.

**DOUG WALKER, CHAIRMAN, REI**

You shouldn't let your friendships get in the way of pursuing the best strategy for the company.

## NICE COMPANY STRATEGY: Standing in the Spotlight

The "spotlight" is a point of acknowledgment that places individuals at the center of attention. Success has, in some way, warranted special consideration. Many will be gratified and edified by the proverbial pat on the back, the "Atta boy!" and the "Great job!" Overly nice guys, however, may be embarrassed by excessive attention or simply be too shy to stand in the spotlight. They might view any "formal" recognition as crass or grandstanding, giving it a negative connotation in their minds.

At a superficial level, business leaders may notice this aversion and just write it off, feeling grateful for one less thing to worry about. However, it would be shortsighted and misguided to think that overly nice guys don't want to be acknowledged at all. They simply want to be acknowledged for their contributions in different and meaningful ways. By acknowledging them in a genuine fashion, you will inspire overly nice guys to be more creative, more assertive, and to tap their true potential while going for more "wins." If you don't recognize them, overly nice guys will likely feel unappreciated. This can lead to other, more serious ramifications, such as disconnecting from their responsibilities, leaving the company, or, perhaps, suffering through a bout or two of Nice Guy Whiplash.

Yet when the *right* spotlight shines upon a nice guy, everyone benefits. Identifying the right type of spotlight is the challenge. Here are three strategies to aid with this task:

1. *Putting on the Right Lens.* Take the time to understand what is (and what is not) important for each overly nice guy on your team. If recognition comes in the form of two tickets to a baseball game with no word ever said to anyone, do it. If another overly nice guy has been part of a team and believes that the entire team played an important role in his success, then acknowledge the

team as a whole in an appropriate way. At Ross Perot's company, EDS, managers were instructed to ask their people for a list of "prizes" for each of their subordinates. Each prize was associated with a specific value and, depending upon the size of the win, a correlating prize was given. With a creative and open mind—and open communication—you can shine the perfect spotlight on every winner in your group.

2. *Ignore Credit Grabbers.* Credibility is lost when attention is lavished upon Credit Grabbers—people who seek the spotlight but do not deserve it. Nice guys tend to have a high level of authenticity and perceptiveness around these things, and they usually loathe these people. Knowingly shining a spotlight on them negates the value of the spotlight.

3. *Formality Required.* There are times when you must formally recognize overly nice guys for their winning contributions. In these cases, the win becomes an important instrument to demonstrate competencies, perseverance, and creativity. It legitimizes their contributions and sets the stage for others to aspire to reach high levels of achievement. When this takes place, it is important to explain to the overly nice guy that the spotlight is necessary because of the positive impact it will have on others.

The symbiotic relationship between healthy competition and the spotlight sets the stage for overly nice guys to win, to make a difference, and to tap their potential. By winning they are positively impacting themselves, their coworkers, their companies, and, potentially, the world. In the words of Joe McGuire of Tweeter Home Entertainment Group, "Most people want to come to work and they want to succeed. They want to be useful. And they want to be viewed as a contributor."

*Chapter Summary*

## NICE GUY MOTIVES AND SYMPTOMS

| | |
|---|---|
| **Deference to Others** | Overly nice guys have an unfortunate habit of deferring to others when it comes to winning. They'd often prefer to see others get ahead, even when it may be *their* work that really made the difference. |
| **Reluctance to Create Losers** | If an overly nice guy's winning is going to create a loser, they often prefer to avoid the competition. Unfortunately, this also means that great ideas may not surface. |
| **Diminishing Oneself** | Allowing others to win, overly nice guys ultimately diminish their value and their ideas. |

## NICE GUY STRATEGIES

| | |
|---|---|
| **Failure** | As fearful of failure as overly nice guys typically are, it is important that they recognize its importance and learn how to grow from it. In so doing, they will be much more likely to win in bigger ways in the future. |
| **Excellence** | Overly nice guys must learn to value the very best ideas, especially if those ideas are theirs. To defer one's own winning ideas so that others don't lose is irresponsible. |
| **Recognition** | Overly nice guys must learn that receiving recognition for a job well done is not only okay but extremely important. By avoiding recognition, the importance of their ideas and contributions is prevented from being fully realized. |

### NICE COMPANY STRATEGIES

| | |
|---|---|
| **Healthy Competition** | When people compete in a healthy way, better ideas are forged. Those ideas often turn into winning solutions that benefit the entire organization. |
| **Standing in the Spotlight** | Don't assume that all nice guys desire the same type of recognition. Make sure you learn what does and does not appeal to them, and plan out your recognition programs accordingly. |

AFTERWORD

You have a call to action. You have the right to succeed and to remain nice. You can be strong and assertive without becoming a
jerk. You have strategies that can help you succeed. You must now
take responsibility for your success.

It is our wish that these concepts resonate with you. While we
don't expect that you'll absorb and act on every story, strategy, and
experience related in this book, we do hope that they will provide
perspective on how to tackle many of the problems associated with
Nice Guy Syndrome in business.

And as you boldly go forward, remember to take it step-by-step;
that you can optimize your strengths; that you can fail and re-
cover; and that you can speak up, confront, and achieve anything
that you set your mind to. And in so doing, you and your organization will win in new and wonderful ways.

If you'll indulge us, we'd like to end with one more story . . .

# Seven Marbles—The Question

One CEO asked, "If you were negotiating the distribution of seven valuable marbles between you and a colleague, and you could not break the marbles in half, and both of you were equally well off from an economic perspective, how many marbles would you take for yourself?"

## Seven Marbles—The Answer

If you take six or seven, you're behaving like a jerk.

If you take zero, one, or two, read this book again, as you are still too nice.

If you take four or five, you are well balanced, but you are not thinking about the long term.

And if you take three, consider yourself "effectively nice."

## Why?

Selecting three marbles brings you as close to balance as possible. As for the fourth marble, if you are economically well off—or at least proportionally balanced relative to your counterpart—it behooves you to let him or her keep the fourth marble. In doing so, you set a precedent that demonstrates that you are willing to invest in a longer-term relationship by giving the marble away. The benefits that come from such an investment may be tangible returns that come back to you, acts of altruism, or a combination of both. What is critical to remember is that you remain effectively nice and balanced in the marble distribution, and that you are keenly aware of your situation as well as your counterpart's. Had you been poor and your opponent wealthy, the number of marbles taken may have been different.

## Who?

Joe O'Donnell, founder and CEO of the Boston Culinary Group—with more than twenty thousand employees worldwide—shared his Seven Marbles story with us and reflected upon the experiences that shaped his selection of the number of marbles to be taken. As a provider of food services for ski areas, O'Donnell struck a deal with the owner of a ski mountain. At the end of the season both made out well, but the distribution of profit was disproportionately high in O'Donnell's favor due to the previously agreed-upon terms and conditions. After evaluating the disparity, O'Donnell elected to share his profits with his partner, an act that he felt was the right thing to do (even though he had no contractual obligation to do so). O'Donnell gave his partner the fourth marble. And while it took a few hundred thousand dollars from his pocket, his kind act has come back to him over and over again, as he has been recognized as a smart, successful, honorable, and nice businessperson. By the way, thirty years later O'Donnell still provides the food services at the mountain resort.

Be Nice, Be Effective, and Be Successful! And the corner office will someday be yours, because you have become a strong, balanced, and effective leader.

## Acknowledgments

We are grateful to the many people who contributed to the development of the "nice guy" concept in general and to this book in particular.

We could not have written this book without the many CEOs and thought leaders who shared their time and insight with us. Thanks to each and every one of you. And many thanks to the dozens of friends and peers whose stories helped illuminate the challenges that nice guys face in the business world. We will always be grateful for your courage, honesty, and willingness to share your experiences with us.

Thanks to Jack and Suzy Welch and Tom Peters, who provided inspiration and direction in the early days. We are indebted to the good folks at the *Harvard Business Review*—especially Bronwyn Fryer, Julia Kirby, and Ellen Peebles—who provided the opportunity to write an article for *HBR* and were invaluable in helping us hone our concept and give it legs. We are very grateful to our literary agent, Jill Marsal of the Dijkstra Literary Agency, who saw the potential for a book, reached out to us, and encouraged the creation of a book proposal. Her ability to shepherd us through the process was indispensable. Thank you to Adrian Zackheim, Jeffrey Krames, Allison McLean, and everyone at Portfolio for their enthusiasm and willingness to take a chance on us. And much gratitude to our publicist, Barbara Cave Henricks, for enthusiastically joining the Nice Guy movement and helping us get the word out to the masses.

Thanks to Rebecca Lucy for her help with the design of the nice guy surveys and the analysis of the data. A big thank-you to Laura Bayko, Russ's office manager, for being such a huge help with all of the administrative details. And many thanks to Jack Fox, Jack Santos, Deirdre Girard, Rob Quintal, Robin Cecil, Julie Ganong, David Hoag, Mike Kraine, Jon Mysel, Mike Scarpone, Ross Knights, Socorro Ortega, Jackie Woodside, Lisa Paden, Madeline Sherwood, Denise DeSimone, David Ray, Vern Butler, and Mitch Roberts for their contributions and support. Additional thanks to the ACK Forum, Vern Harnish, and the participants of the April 2007 EO Advanced Business Conference for their valuable input. We would also like to send a special thanks to Leigh Hafrey, Steve Weissman, and Kate Dobson for their assistance and support. There were many more of you—too numerous to mention—who helped us in so many ways. You know who you are, and we want you to know you are truly appreciated.

On a personal note, Russ would like to thank Jasmin for her critical thinking and "tough love support"—it made the difference! And much thanks again to Jasmin, Justin, and Aaron for their patience. He personally dedicates this book to his beloved dad, Allen, one of the original nice guys who is no longer with us. Russ would also like to acknowledge Professor Andrew Downie, who started him down the road to writing.

Tim sends love and gratitude to his parents, who always said that "if you can't say anything nice, don't say anything at all" and showed him how to live with integrity through the ups and downs of life. He is also grateful to his close friends, who have taught him so much about the deeper meaning of "nice" and been so supportive during the process of creating this book.

Chuck would like to thank his family, Karen, Chris, and Katy, and his parents, brothers, and other extended family members, for their many valuable demonstrations of how we can effectively be both nice and authentic. Finally, he thanks his many colleagues and friends who have provided inspiration and motivation to try to help make the world a better place, one genuinely and assertively nice step at a time.